# Dividing New Mexico's Waters, 1700–1912

# Dividing New Mexico's Waters, 1700–1912

John O. Baxter

**University of New Mexico Press**

Albuquerque

© 1997 by the University of New Mexico Press
First Edition

Library of Congress Cataloging-in-Publication Data

Baxter, John O., 1927–
    Dividing New Mexico's waters, 1700–1912 / John O. Baxter. —
1st ed.
        p.   cm.
    ISBN 0-8263-1747-2 (cloth)
    1. Water resources development—New Mexico—History.   I.
Title.
  HD1694.N6B39   1996
  333.91′009789—dc20                                        95-50235

# Contents

# List of Illustrations

# Preface

ALTHOUGH NEW MEXICANS now face a number of difficult environmental problems, none of them receives more attention than our water supply. Located in a semiarid region with limited precipitation, New Mexico is extremely vulnerable to water shortages. During the last few decades, population growth and urban development have intensified competition for available supplies. Each day, demand increases from agricultural, industrial, domestic, and recreational users, seemingly without concern for the future. News media report proposals for a new golf course or computer chip factory, each one requiring staggering amounts of water. As the struggle continues, lawsuits to determine rights to surface and ground water fill the dockets of state and federal courts. Clearly, the situation is precarious.

Despite the flood of recent publicity, disputes to determine water ownership are not new to New Mexico, but have recurred frequently during the state's long history. For centuries, governmental officials under Spanish, Mexican, and United States administrations have wrestled with water apportionment issues and related problems, particularly in times of drought. In the past, as now, authorities searched for ways to share recurrent shortages in keeping with the accepted values of the community. Frequently, their attempts to allocate scanty resources failed to satisfy any of the contending parties. Nevertheless, the solutions imposed provide material for an intriguing history worthy of consideration today.

This book discusses the evolution of water administration in New Mexico from the colonial era through the first decade of the twentieth century. Based on archival sources from the Spanish, Mexican, and Territorial periods, the research begins with documents created during the reconquest of the province by Spanish forces in 1693–1694. (Unfortunately, almost all records from the seventeenth century were destroyed during the Pueblo Revolt of 1680.) With New Mexico a crown colony once again, the settlers reestablished an agrarian-pastoral society based on grants of land from the royal domain. Because agriculture was virtually impossible without irrigation, officials placed great emphasis on water availability when they distributed lands to establish new communities. As the settlements took root, Hispano farmers devised a practical system for managing and maintaining their community acequias. Conflicts for water were inevitable, and, in this work, records from lawsuits serve as case studies of the resolution of irrigation controversies. Although disputes concerning water allocation, ditch repairs, flood damage, and right-of-way arose frequently, local officials usually arranged solutions based on recognized customs and common sense rather than legal abstractions.

As it matured during the colonial and Mexican periods, the community acequia became generally accepted as the basis for water administration in New Mexico. After the United States conquest of 1846, Hispanos managed to retain the same procedures for a few decades. Control of the Territorial legislature and county offices allowed continuation of customary means for water management and distribution. Changes came rapidly after 1878 when rail transportation linked New Mexico to the national economy for the first time. Eastern promoters initiated large-scale irrigation projects that promised quick economic growth. Unavoidably, their demands for water clashed with the needs of subsistence farmers, who had formed the predominant element in the territorial population until then. In 1907, New Mexico's legislature passed a comprehensive code of water laws, a legal milestone that marked the beginning of centralized control of hydro resources. Although lawmakers intended to protect the community acequia and other traditional institutions, after 1907, water policy became increasingly dominated by the prevailing Anglo culture. It is to be hoped that a consideration of water administration as it evolved during New Mexico's long and dry history may provide fresh insight into the problems that continue up to the present day.

# 1 | Water and Settlement Patterns

Water has always been a precious commodity in New Mexico. From the remote past to recent times, most New Mexicans have supported themselves by tilling the soil. In a semiarid region such as the Southwest, where agriculture usually depends on irrigation, careful use of available water has been the key to survival. When Spanish conquistadors led by Francisco Vásquez de Coronado first arrived in 1540, they found Pueblo Indians at Zuñi subsisting on crops of corn, beans, and squash. Coronado believed that the Zuñis worshipped water as a god, "because it makes the maize grow and sustains their life." Accustomed to aridity in the mother country and New Spain, the invaders found such beliefs unremarkable. Soon after the arrival of Juan de Oñate's colonizing expedition in 1598, the Spaniards began constructing an irrigation canal to serve their nascent settlement. Later governors also recognized the importance of evaluating water supplies prior to the establishment of new communities. Although New Mexico possessed vast land reserves, lack of exploitable streams made many areas unsuitable for farming. As competition for water increased with population growth, citizens, as individuals and in groups, attempted to preempt hydro resources for themselves, sometimes at the expense of other Hispanos or Pueblo Indians. Thus, availability of water proved to be an important element in determining settlement patterns and economic and social relations in colonial New Mexico. Land grant records and other archives provide rich sources that demonstrate the significance of water in the region's early history.

Hispano colonization of New Mexico began in 1598, when don Juan de Oñate led a large expedition out of San Bartolomé in present Chihuahua to establish a permanent settlement on the upper Rio Grande. Composed of 10 Franciscan friars and 129 hopeful citizen-soldiers, many with families, the party set out in January accompanied by livestock, pack animals, and baggage carts that spread over the countryside for more than a league (2.6 miles). After an arduous journey, Oñate's advance guard had reached the area above today's Española by July 11. There, at the junction of the Rio Grande and the Rio Chama, the Spaniards established headquarters at the Pueblo Indian village of Ohke, which they renamed San Juan Bautista. Following a round of visits to several nearby pueblos, including Picurís, Taos, San Ildefonso, Pecos, and Jémez the colonists began to settle in at San Juan in characteristic fashion. Assisted by 1,500 "barbarous Indians," Oñate's followers started to build an acequia, a necessary first step in founding a city, to be called San Francisco de los Españoles.[1] Somewhat premature, the new community failed to materialize, but the ditch project clearly demonstrated the importance of securing a reliable water supply for agricultural and domestic purposes. Although not always explicit, the same concern manifested itself in the development of subsequent settlements throughout New Mexico.

Crowded and disease-ridden, Ohke soon proved unsatisfactory, causing the colonists to find new quarters across the Rio Grande on the west bank. Sometime before Christmas 1600, they set up residence in the partially abandoned pueblo of Yunque, which they called San Gabriel. Once again the settlers lost no time in establishing an irrigation system. A leading church historian, Fray Juan de Torquemada, described the arrangement thus: "San Gabriel . . . is situated between two rivers, and with water from the smaller [the Chama], they irrigate wheat, barley, corn, and other things that they plant in gardens."[2]

As in other regions of colonial Mexico, Spaniards in New Mexico disdained native corn except in emergencies; wheat became their staple food grain—a crop seldom grown in New Spain without irrigation.[3]

Although Torquemada's account indicated an auspicious beginning for farmers at San Gabriel, the new colony soon faced serious problems. Not long after arriving, Oñate wrote enthusiastically about the wonders of his conquest to New Spain's viceroy, the Count of Monterrey. Describing Pueblo Indian crops, he proudly declared that, "Their corn and vegetables . . . are the best and largest . . . in the world." Subsequently, other expedition members praised the skills of native farmers, recalling that they produced bumper crops of corn, cotton, beans, squash, and melons. Some fields were irrigated; others depended on seasonal rainfall.[4]

In fact, except for Indian surpluses, procured by purchase or extortion, the New Mexico colony probably would not have survived its first winter. Contrary to Oñate's glowing reports, his followers experienced grave difficulties in adjusting to frontier life. Their strident complaints to authorities in Mexico City caused Oñate to fall from favor and face a long investigation. During the inquiry in 1601, officials collected depositions from Oñate's adherents and detractors, many of whom had already fled to the south. Although contradictory, their statements comprise the only source for evaluating Hispano agriculture in this early period.

Witnesses who favored the proud *adelantado* asserted that wheat harvests had increased significantly each year. According to Captain Alonso Gómez Montesinos, the settlers had planted a mere seven fanegas in 1599, which produced 188 fanegas (300 bushels) of grain, a yield of almost twenty-seven to one. In the next two years, wheat harvests had risen to 800, and then 1,500, fanegas, allowing the colony to subsist with only a small supplement of Indian corn.

Alférez Martín Gómez agreed, and swore that with fourteen Indians and sufficient plowshares he could provide bread for the entire colony and have a large surplus available for the native population.

Oñate's opponents, however, told a different story. One former settler summed up New Mexico's climatic extremes with the phrase, "*ocho meses de invierno y quatro de infierno* (eight months of winter and four months of hell)." Other former colonists declared that chronic drought conditions inhibited agriculture in the new province. Furthermore, the newcomers' continuing demands for food had depleted native reserves to the point that Spaniards and Indians alike faced starvation.[5] Unfortunately, neither side provided evidence concerning the all-important irrigation system.

After weighing the testimony, Monterrey's successor, Viceroy Luis de Velasco II, decided that the settlement's agricultural problems were not insurmountable. More significant, he resolved to maintain New Mexico as a crown colony supported by royal subsidies in order to continue the missionary effort among indigenous tribes. Oñate failed to redeem himself, however. On August 24, 1607, he resigned as New Mexico's governor and was replaced by Pedro de Peralta who, following a long delay, arrived at his post early in 1610. Acting on orders from the viceroy, Peralta immediately laid out a new capital city, La Villa de Santa Fe, which symbolized a fresh start for the beleaguered province. Velasco's detailed *instrucción* directed the governor to lay out a central plaza and choose locations for public buildings; newly appointed municipal officials had responsibility for distributing lots for houses and gardens to each citizen. The viceroy's order also authorized every resident to receive four caballerías of land (about 400 acres) and sufficient water for irrigation, but the realities of the location probably limited the allotments to smaller amounts.[6] For the townsite, Peralta chose a small valley bisected by a reliable stream that tumbled out of the lofty Sangre de Cristo Mountains as it flowed west toward the Rio Grande. Dubbed the Rio de Santa Fe, the river provided enough water to irrigate farmlands on each bank in normal years, although the villa's population eventually outstripped the stream's resources.

## The Early Acequia System

Because seventeenth-century New Mexico's local records were almost entirely destroyed in the Pueblo Revolt of 1680, we know very little concerning development of Santa Fe's early acequia system. Accounts of the great Indian uprising indicate plowed fields south of the Santa Fe River near the chapel of San Miguel.[7] Hispano farmers probably irrigated these lands from the Acequia Madre, the city's most important southside ditch, which continues in use today. Before the revolt, the villa's citizens had also built an acequia into the plaza area north of the river for domestic purposes and watering livestock. When the

Indian attack first hit Santa Fe on August 13, 1680, the Pueblos cut off the defenders' water supply by blocking that ditch. As their thirst increased under a broiling summer sun, the Spaniards soon decided to abandon the city and begin the long retreat to the El Paso area.[8]

Twelve years later, during his preliminary reconnaissance of New Mexico, the redoubtable Governor Diego de Vargas, hero of the reconquest, employed the same tactics when he arrived at Santa Fe in September 1692. Finding the Pueblos firmly entrenched in the villa and reluctant to admit him, Vargas ordered five men to close off the same acequia, forcing the natives to come to terms.[9] On both occasions, control of the water supply determined the outcome of the siege.

Having secured grudging acquiescence from the Pueblos for the reimposition of Spanish rule during his first *entrada*, Vargas returned to El Paso eager to organize permanent reoccupation of New Mexico. As news of the proposed recolonization spread, some of the old settlers asked for revalidation of title to their ancestral properties, long before plans had been completed for the return home. In January 1693, the crusty veteran, Sargento Mayor Juan Lucero de Godoy, who had served the king for fifty-two of his sixty-nine years, requested lands "two harquebus shots" from Santa Fe that he had occupied with his large family before the revolt. With the cautious proviso that there be no "damage to any third party with a better right," Vargas gave tentative approval. After the villa's recapture, during the first difficult planting season Lucero generously loaned part of his fields to various landless friends and relatives, including his mother-in-law, Bernardina de Salas, his *compadre,* Captain Alonso Rael de Aguilar, Captain Fernando Durán y Chaves, and the Franciscan, Fray Antonio Obregón. On April 7, 1695, Lucero received permanent title from his commander, Governor Vargas.[10]

Later, Vargas made a similar concession to Maestre de Campo Roque de Madrid, another seasoned campaigner who figured prominently in the long struggle to recover the province. Before leaving El Paso, Madrid petitioned for a house and lands next to Santa Fe formerly owned by his parents and grandparents. Like the Luceros, the Madrid family had been prominent residents of the capital almost since its founding. Again, Vargas quickly approved, recognizing Madrid's many years of loyal service as he did so.[11] Subsequently, he made similar grants of house sites, garden plots, and farmlands to Luis Maese, Domingo Martín, and other returnees in March 1695.[12] Since agricultural land close to the villa was limited, Vargas and his successor, Pedro Rodríguez Cubero, restricted grants to *una media fanega de sembradura de maíz* (one-half fanega of planting land for corn),[13] a quantity deemed adequate to support an average-sized family. None of the granting documents issued during this period refer to water for irrigation or any other purpose.

When Vargas left El Paso in October 1693, his followers numbered about

800 persons, including 100 soldiers and 70 colonizing families.[14] Realizing that he needed many more settlers to hold the province and prevent a recurrence of the 1680 disaster, the governor undertook a vigorous recruiting campaign in the interior of New Spain. His efforts received support from Viceroy Conde de Galve, who offered to pay expenses for families in Mexico City willing to relocate to New Mexico. Some sixty-odd households volunteered for the expedition. Led by Fray Francisco Farfán, they entered Santa Fe on June 23, 1694 after a journey of nine months.[15]

In the following year, Vargas's trusted subordinate, Juan Páez Hurtado, organized a second party of forty-four families at Zacatecas. They arrived at New Mexico's capital on May 9.[16] To provide homesites and farmlands for the newcomers, Vargas decided to establish a new villa in the area known as La Cañada, a fertile, well-watered valley about twenty miles north of Santa Fe.[17] In choosing the site and planning the new community to be built there, the governor showed particular concern for the availability of irrigation water. The first major cession from the royal domain made after the Pueblo Revolt, the Santa Cruz grant merits consideration since it demonstrated important aspects of future Spanish land policy in New Mexico.

During the seventeenth century, Spanish pioneers had established a series of ranchos and haciendas along La Cañada extending east from the Rio Grande to Chimayó. After the retreat to El Paso, Tano Indians from the pueblos of San Lázaro and San Cristóbal in the Galisteo Basin moved into the valley to avoid a growing threat from Apache raiders. Once located, the Indians built new pueblo villages and took over fields and acequias abandoned by their former foes. Determined to reclaim the valley for Hispano settlement, Vargas, early in 1695, ordered the Tanos to vacate their recently constructed villages. For residents of San Cristóbal, he designated new lands near Chimayó; San Lázaro's occupants were told to go to the nearby pueblo of San Juan. Angered by their sudden displacement, both Tano groups joined the renewed Pueblo uprising in 1696. After the restoration of peace, some moved into various Tewa villages; others eventually returned to Galisteo.[18]

With the Tanos out of the way, Vargas issued a proclamation on April 19, 1695 founding "*La Villa Nueva de Santa Cruz de la Cañada de Españoles-Mexicanos del Rey Nuestro Señor Carlos Segundo* (the New Villa of Santa Cruz de la Cañada of Mexican Spaniards for the King Our Lord Charles II)." The document indicated that San Lázaro had been evacuated and would be reoccupied by the sixty families from Mexico City that had arrived the year before. In the grant, Vargas placed particular emphasis on water for irrigation and the necessary means for its diversion and distribution:

> I designate the said pueblo, its dwelling houses with its lands cleared for farming, drains, irrigation ditches, and dam or dams that the said native Indians

had and have for their irrigation and certainty of gathering crops; in addition, I designate and make a grant in name of His Majesty of their diversions (*sacas*) of water that have been discovered and that they may discover, their forests, pastures, cañadas which the said natives enjoyed, without damage to the haciendas and ranchos that fall within their ownership and district.[19]

Reflecting a fundamental principle of Spanish jurisprudence, the reference to interested third parties protected any returning pre-revolt occupants.

On April 21, the governor personally escorted the villa's first citizens out of Santa Fe over the familiar trail to the vacated pueblo, which was located south of the river opposite present Santa Cruz plaza. After placing the settlers in possession of the town site, Vargas directed that each family receive enough land to plant one-half fanega of corn, the same amount commonly distributed in Santa Fe.[20] The limitation suggests a desire to prevent concentration of large landholdings in the hands of a few, and provide later arrivals with means to support themselves.

During May 1696, Santa Cruz did receive additional settlers—nineteen family heads, including several bachelors and widowers, who had arrived a year earlier with the Zacatecas colonists. In a decree authorizing them to move, Vargas expressed concern that Santa Fe lacked sufficient irrigation water to produce food for the large population congregated there. A more promising situation prevailed at Santa Cruz, where fertile land, easily irrigated, remained unoccupied. With becoming modesty, the governor also observed that he had greatly improved the new villa's irrigation system by subsidizing necessary maintenance and repairs from his own pocket.[21] Soon after arriving, the settlers built (or refurbished) an acequia near the abandoned pueblo of San Cristóbal, about five miles upstream from Santa Cruz at present La Puebla. Landowners later identified the ditch mouth as a boundary call in a deed of sale, *la toma de las familias Mexicanas* (the intake of the Mexican families), probably located at the head of today's Sombrillo acequia.[22]

Vargas worked hard to rebuild New Mexico and restore peace to the region, but he encountered serious difficulties. Less than a month after the Zacatecas settlers arrived at Santa Cruz, the Pueblo Indians again rose in revolt. Believing that their lands had been usurped, the nearby Tewas and Tanos particularly resented establishment of the Santa Cruz settlement. Discouraged and fearful, many of the villa's citizens sought permission to relocate in a more favorable location or return to Mexico City. Strongly opposed to any retreat, the governor withheld approval, but agreed to forward the requests to the viceroy, who took no action.[23]

After six months of fighting, Vargas managed to defeat the Pueblos, but by that time, his tour of duty as New Mexico's governor had ended. On July 2, 1697, Pedro Rodríguez Cubero arrived in Santa Fe with authorization from the viceroy to take charge of provincial administration. Following his arrival,

Rodríguez Cubero joined forces with dissident members of Santa Fe's *cabildo* (municipal council) against Vargas—a struggle for power that resulted in imprisonment of the latter for three years. Finally, in the summer of 1700, the hero of the reconquest obtained his release and journeyed to Mexico City, where he was completely exonerated. On November 10, 1703, he returned to New Mexico and resumed the governorship.[24]

Soon after arriving, Vargas found that conditions at Santa Cruz had deteriorated badly during his absence. To determine appropriate action, Vargas made an official inspection of the Santa Cruz-Chimayó area early in 1704. The rapid approach of the planting season gave urgency to his journey. In a report dated February 13, the governor described conditions as deplorable. At Santa Cruz, the plaza had been moved from the site originally chosen by Vargas; only six families had houses at the new location. Some citizens lived nearby on lands granted to them, but others had become homeless after selling the one-half fanega parcels received in 1695. A few property owners, both pre-revolt settlers and newcomers from Mexico City, had enlarged their holdings by purchases from neighbors. Following a review of each person's condition, Vargas revalidated individual holdings on the basis of original grant or subsequent purchase. For those without land, he made new grants to twenty-four petitioners, including six widows whose husbands had succumbed in recent combat or from illness.[25] Despite a shaky beginning, Santa Cruz developed as a settled community of self-sufficient, irrigated farms after Vargas's second land distribution and the restoration of peace.

During the Indian uprising of 1696, all the Tewa pueblos north of Santa Fe had joined the insurgents except Tesuque. At San Ildefonso, rebels burned the mission buildings before fleeing to the mountains west of the Rio Grande; dissidents also killed four Spaniards in Nambé's churchyard. Residents of Pojoaque, Jacona, and Cuyamungué abandoned their villages and took refuge with other Tewas or among the Navajos. In 1707, more than a decade later, Governor Francisco Cuervo y Valdés reestablished the pueblo of Pojoaque by persuading some Indian families to return home.[26] Indian occupants did not return to the other two villages, however, creating an irresistible opportunity for land-hungry Hispanos to take over the irrigated fields. Beginning in 1699, Governor Rodríguez Cubero had made a series of moderate-sized land grants in the Pojoaque Valley, chiefly to veterans of the recent conflict. Situated midway between Santa Fe and Santa Cruz, they strengthened New Mexico's northern frontier by filling the gap between the two villas. Although Cubero did not found a new town as Vargas had done at Santa Cruz, the resulting settlement pattern proved similar—a scattering of individual ranchos along the river. As population increased, the rancheros developed an irrigation system and sought ways to allocate water among themselves and the Tewa villages. Almost immediately, these grants caused friction that led to lengthy litigation with Indian neighbors, and the issue of equitable distribution of the valley's limited water resources remains unresolved even today.

Beneficiaries of Cubero's largess included a young Spanish soldier, Captain Ignacio de Roybal y Torrado, who had served honorably during the reconquest. Born near the famous shrine of Compostela in Galicia, Roybal came to the New World and fought beside Vargas in the campaign to recover New Mexico for the Spanish crown. When hostilities ended, don Ignacio and his bride, the daughter of an important pre-revolt family, settled permanently at Jacona, where he amassed a substantial estate. His success as a powerful landholder represented a goal to which many New Mexicans aspired in the eighteenth century. Sometime in 1699, Cubero granted most of the Jacona lands to Roybal's brother-in-law, Jacinto Peláez, also from Spain, who died within a few years. On December 6, 1699, the governor conveyed an adjoining three fanegas of farmland to Juan de Mestas, a Santa Fe native who had returned from El Paso in 1693. After Peláez died, Cubero granted his Jacona lands to Roybal, kinsman of the deceased, on October 2, 1702. Three years later, don Ignacio became the area's leading landowner by trading a good traveling horse (*un caballo de camino bueno*) to Mestas for the west portion of the latter's land, a tract that extended from the Rio Cuyamungué (Tesuque) to Peláez's grant. Only 1.5 fanegas of corn land lay within the purchase, but wording in the deed authorized the buyer to break out a larger area for planting if he so desired—a stipulation approved by the attending alcalde.[27]

Prior to exercising his right, Roybal petitioned Governor Juan Domingo de Bustamante for a clarification of his title in 1723, more than two decades after buying the property. To avoid misunderstandings and costly litigation, he asked that the governor require Mestas to present his grant papers so that boundaries might be measured and landmarks set. At the same time, Roybal made a bold attempt to secure official authorization for sufficient water from the Cuyamungué to assure regular irrigation of his fields. In a document unprecedented in New Mexico, he "registered" an unspecified portion of the river's flow (*rexistro una toma de agua del dho río para el beneficio y regadía de dhos tierras*).[28] At first, Bustamante ignored the request for water, although he did order Mestas to produce documentation for his grant. Not to be denied, Roybal wrote again to the governor two years later, seeking approval for an acequia from the Cuyamungué. Citing the needs of his large family and his years of military service, don Ignacio explained that he wished to plant an additional five or six fanegas of corn on the Mestas lands—a big increase of about forty or fifty acres. After referring to the clause allowing such an enlargement, he assured Bustamante that the ditch would cause no damage to anyone with a better right—an important consideration in making grants of land or water. This time the governor acknowledged Roybal's petition and gave him a license for the new ditch.[29]

Known today as La Acequia Larga de Jacona, the ditch still runs across the lands farmed by Ignacio de Roybal in the early 1700s.

While Roybal and his neighbors made themselves at home at Pojoaque and Jacona, other Hispanos searched out suitable locations for irrigated farms and pasture lands to sustain their families. Despite intermittent hostilities with surrounding Indian tribes, they left the safety of Santa Fe for various parts of the Rio Grande Valley and its tributaries. At the turn of the century, settlers returned to pre-revolt communities to the south at Bernalillo, Alameda, and Atrisco. In 1706, Governor Francisco Cuervo y Valdés founded a new villa on the river's east bank, which he named in honor of the Duke of Alburquerque, New Spain's viceroy at the time. In the next decades, the line of settlement gradually extended south to the Belén-Tomé area. To the north, frontiersmen pushed beyond Santa Cruz and Chimayó to lay out scattered placitas on the Rio Grande above present Española and along the Rio Chama near Oñate's San Gabriel. In the late 1720s, Hispano farmers and stockmen, ignoring the obvious risk of Comanche incursions, moved into the Taos Valley, which became New Mexico's northern frontier. Blessed with abundant water resources, the region proved particularly well adapted for irrigated wheat production.

As New Mexico's population grew, there was an even faster increase in livestock holdings, causing ranchers to search out new pastures away from the Rio Grande. At midcentury, adventurous Albuquerque residents looked covetously at the next watershed to the west, the Rio Puerco, seeing it as a place suitable for expansion. Although the Navajo regarded that country as their own, the Puerco Valley offered enough water for some irrigated farming and many leagues of grazing on the hills adjacent. In the autumn of 1753, six hopeful settlers, including Bernabé Montaño and four of his brothers, submitted a formal petition to Governor Tomás Vélez Cachupín for unoccupied lands on the Puerco. Specifically referring to the need for reliable irrigation, the petitioners said they had found a tract "which always retains a little water that is continuous (*que siempre arestado asi poca el agua que tiene continua*)." After recalling valiant service by fathers and grandfathers against "infidel enemies," they complained of present poverty so egregious that they survived only by weeding corn or gathering firewood for nearby Indian pueblos in exchange for food. Mounted and armed for protection, the settlers expected to better their material condition and to increase tithe payments to the church. On October 23, Vélez Cachupín ordered Antonio Baca, alcalde mayor of Santa Ana, Zía, and Jémez to inspect the site and determine how many families might be successfully accommodated there. Concerned about irrigation, the governor particularly wanted to know if the projected farms could be watered by damming the Rio Puerco.[30] Accompanied by two "experts" in agricultural matters, Baca rode over to the Puerco for a careful investigation before reporting enthusiastically to his superior. In addition to unlimited pasture, the valley had adequate timber for construction and firewood. As for farming, all agreed that the petitioners could easily establish productive fields by building a dam for diversion and storage, and taking out an acequia, tasks familiar to all New Mexicans. Optimistically, the three officials decided that, in times of shortage, the settlers might supplement their needs with crops raised on dry land (*siembras de temporal*). Impressed by their appraisal, Vélez Cachupín authorized the founding of a new plaza that he called Nuestra Señora de la Luz, San Fernando y San Blas, a grandiose title honoring the reigning monarch, Fernando VI, as well as two important figures from church iconography. He suggested that the original petitioners enlist additional families to bring their number to twelve. Conforming to official government procedure, the governor laid down several important conditions for the settlement:

1. Pastures, woodlands, and watering places must remain common for the use of all
2. Individual ownership must be confined to the farmlands allocated to each family in equal segments
3. As a defensive measure against raids by "barbarous Apaches," the house lots allocated to the grantees must be contiguous, forming a square plaza with a single entrance large enough for carts—an arrangement much safer than scattered settlement
4. All citizens must work together in building houses, laying out the plaza, damming the river, and digging the necessary acequias
5. To obtain clear title, the settlers must occupy their lands for four years

As ordered by Vélez, Baca gathered the grantees on December 11 at the approved site in the windswept Puerco Valley to take them through the ancient ceremony of possession. Grasping the hand of Bernabé Montaño, their leader, the alcalde led him over the lands, stopping occasionally to pull up tufts of grass or throw a few stones, while everyone cried in unison, "Long live King Fernando VI!" Baca concluded the ritual by designating well-known landmarks as the outer boundaries of the grant. Three months later, on March 11, 1754, just before spring planting began, all interested parties reassembled at the site of the tiny settlement for the distribution of individual house lots and tracts of farmland, which measured 100 by 300 *varas* (a vara = 33.6 inches). Before riding off, Baca advised the settlers that they had secured title to all resources in the grant, adding that, to succeed, they must cooperate wholeheartedly in plowing fields and building an irrigation system, the basic infrastructure for an agricultural community.[31] For two decades, the citizens of Nuestra Señora de la Luz, San Fernando y San Blas farmed and ranched at their outpost on the Puerco and fought furiously with various later arrivals concerning the location of grant boundaries. In the 1770s, however, all the Hispanos left the valley because of pressure from resentful Navajos.[32] A thorough and conscientious executive, Vélez Cachupín demonstrated a similar concern for water issues in other land grants made during his administration. After a personal inspection of the Santa Fe area, the governor concluded that the villa, like Albuquerque, lacked the necessary land and irrigation water to support the growing number of young families congregated there. The province offered few employment opportunities except agriculture and stockraising. Hoping to resolve that problem and erect a barrier against raids from east of the Sangre de Cristos by Plains Indians, he established the frontier plaza of Santo Tomás Apóstol de las Trampas on the west slope of the Sangre de Cristos in 1751. As on the Puerco, the village's founding fathers comprised twelve households; each family received 180 varas for farming, 2,160 varas altogether, that straddled the Rio Trampas. Vélez described the lands as "*todas de regadío y de pan llevar* (all irrigated and for raising wheat)." To accommodate future expansion, the governor also ceded two small cañadas to the south, Los Alamos and Ojo Sarco, recognizing that they were "moist and fertile, although probably not irrigable."[33] Three years later, Vélez Cachupín made another grant at Las Truchas, immediately south of the Las Trampas settlement, to a third group of twelve families, all Espinosas and Romeros, from Chimayó and Pueblo Quemado (Córdova). Three of the latter clan were sons of old Francisco Xavier Romero, one of the Mexico City colonists who had founded the villa of Santa Cruz almost sixty years earlier. The petitioners asked the governor to fulfill a promise to make the Truchas grant as soon as he had determined the boundaries of Las Trampas on the north. Before receiving formal approval, they had planted in the area for two years and had already constructed an irrigation ditch. On March 6, 1754, Vélez approved the grant following the usual inspection, made by Alcalde Juan José Lovato of Santa Cruz. Stipulating conditions similar to those laid down for the Puerco settlement, he named this one Nuestra Señora del Rosario, San Fernando y Santiago, once again genuflecting gracefully to both church and state.

Late in April, as surrounding snowbanks melted, Lovato performed the possession ritual, gave each settler 300 varas of tierra de pan llevar, and designated the outer limits of the grant. On the east, he placed the boundary at "*la toma de la Acequia de el Río del Pueblo quemado que ha de fertilizer esta Poblazón* (the intake of the acequia from the Rio del Pueblo Quemado that must enrich this settlement)."[34] The ditch was probably that referred to in the original petition. Located high in the Sangre de Cristos, it is part of an ingenious arrangement that diverts water from the north fork of the Rio Quemado into the Cañada Cebolla, allowing it to flow down and supplement the meager Rio Truchas. After 250 years, the system remains in use today. The people of Truchas also claimed water rights from the Rito San Leonardo, a small stream that was also coveted by the Trampaseños—a situation that caused heated controversy persisting for many years.

During Vélez Cachupín's first term as governor, Spanish officials saw New Mexico as an important barrier to French expansion into New Spain from bases on the Mississippi to the east. They particularly feared an alliance between encroaching Europeans and Comanches or other aggressive Plains Indian tribes.[35] At the same time, Vélez also realized the need to provide for landless families without means of support. Through his land-grant policy, he attempted to achieve both political and social goals by founding new defensive settlements on the frontiers of the province. Attentive to detail, Vélez recognized the importance of a dependable water source for irrigation, livestock, and the domestic requirements of each new community. Alcaldes, the officials responsible for making investigations of prospective colonization sites, seldom failed to evaluate water conditions in their reports to the governor. Vélez's policies produced mixed results: although the original contingents of twelve families seemed pitifully small, communities like Las Trampas and Las Truchas managed to withstand the Comanche threat; San Fernando on the Rio Puerco fared well enough for twenty years, but Navajo hostility then forced a general retreat from that region.

### Population Growth Presents New Problems

During the second half of the eighteenth century, New Mexico's population continued to grow steadily. In 1776, Fray Francisco Atanasio Domínguez, on an official visit to Franciscan missions in the province, conducted a census of all Hispanos and Pueblo Indians. Excluding the El Paso region, Domínguez tallied a total of 18,344 persons. Spaniards and those of mixed ancestry outnumbered their Pueblo neighbors two to one.[36] To absorb the increase, government officials renewed efforts to accommodate land-hungry citizens in new communities. Determined to expand the perimeter of settlement, Governor Fernando Chacón made several well-placed land grants between 1794 and 1800. These included San Miguel del Vado on the Rio Pecos east of Santa Fe, Cebolleta north of Laguna pueblo on the west, and short-lived Alamillo, down the Rio Grande near present Socorro. In the north, as Comanche raids abated, Chacón approved two important grants in the Taos Valley—the Rio Grande del Rancho in 1795, and Don Fernando de Taos a year later.[37]

The settlement of Cebolleta offered a particularly difficult challenge for Spanish officials. Eager to push New Mexico's western border beyond the Puerco, Chacón recruited thirty families at Albuquerque, receiving from them agreement to found a plaza north of Laguna in a country occupied by Navajos. On March 15, 1800, the hardy pioneers arrived at Cebolleta, their new home. The local alcalde described the place as ideal for settlement, well-endowed with farmland, pasture, and irrigation water. Incensed by the intrusion, nearby Navajos protested at once, but the Hispanos stayed put and began fortifying their village with a stone wall. Open warfare ensued, continuing for five years. Badly outnumbered, the villagers often considered evacuation, but, except for one brief interval, they remained in place on strict orders from Chacón. Reviewing the situation for his superior in Chihuahua (Comandante General Nemesio Salcedo), Chacón explained that he had limited the founding party to thirty "because there is not sufficient water for more (*a cause de no ser suficiente agua para mas*)."[38] Since local conditions prevented Cebolleta from supporting a viable defensive community, the hard-pressed colonists found their interests sacrificed to the larger goal of Spanish expansionism.

In contrast, recipients of the two grants at Taos faced another kind of problem: allocation of limited irrigation water in areas already occupied by other Hispanos or Pueblo Indians. Different strategies emerged in the two situations considered here. Reoccupation of Taos Valley proceeded slowly in the first years after the Vargas reconquest, despite its fertile soil and copious water resources. During the second decade of the eighteenth century, officials at Santa Fe made a few land grants there, although hostile Utes and Comanches frequently raided the area. In 1710, Captain Cristóbal de la Serna, a soldier from the Santa Fe garrison, received a tract of agricultural and grazing land on the Rio de las Trampas (Rio Grande del Rancho) near present Ranchos de Taos. When Serna lost his life during the ill-starred expedition to the buffalo plains led by Lieutenant Governor Pedro de Villasur, his heirs sold the Taos holdings to Diego "El Coyote" Romero, a mixed-blood from the Rio Abajo.[39] Accompanied by his extended family, El Coyote settled on the grant and achieved a measure of prosperity, undaunted by the difficult environment. Together, they pastured livestock, broke out farmland, dug irrigation ditches, and squabbled with their Indian neighbors. In 1742, Romero drew up his last will, itemizing various kinds of farm implements, such as hoes and plowshares, in addition to seven oxen for plowing, twenty-eight horses and mules, eighty cows and calves, and 450 sheep.[40] During the decades after El Coyote's death, Hispano population in Taos Valley increased slowly, numbering only seventy-seven families (331 persons) by 1790.[41] The total included many descendants of the Romero clan who continued to reside on the Serna grant at Ranchos de Taos plaza. As the Comanche menace subsided, the valley looked increasingly attractive to landless New Mexicans, anxious to persuade the appropriate authorities to make new land concessions in underpopulated areas.

Rumors concerning the Rio Grande del Rancho grant provoked controversy even before it was made. Early in 1795, a number of unnamed old settlers from "*el Rancho de Nuestro Padre Francisco del Río de las Trampas* (Ranchos de Taos)" appealed to the Taos alcalde, Antonio José Ortiz, protesting a proposed grant above their fields. Additional irrigation upstream, they said, would inevitably diminish their share of the river's flow and, thus, endanger the livelihood of present landowners. Dutifully, the petitioners added that decreased harvests meant a corresponding decline in tithes and first fruits, so necessary for maintenance of the church. A few days later, the nervous settlers addressed a second request to Ortiz, asking that they themselves receive possession of the lands in question—an appeal approved by Governor Chacón on February 4, 1795.[42] By this bold and unusual maneuver, the grantees thwarted the mysterious outsiders and consolidated their grip on the valley's resources, particularly water from the river.

In 1796, one year after the coup that "locked up" the Rio Grande del Rancho, Chacón authorized the Don Fernando de Taos grant for an area north of the Serna grant bisected by the Rio Fernando. On May 1, Alcalde Ortiz assembled some sixty-odd families on the site and took them through the act of possession. After specifying outer boundaries with the usual landmarks, Ortiz marked off individual tracts for each settler, most of them measuring sixty-three varas in width.[43] Deed records from later years show that, long after the original distribution, Taoseños continued to buy and sell these same sixty-three-vara plots. A year later, in 1797, a number of new arrivals also received lands on the Fernando grant, which quickly became the largest Hispano community in Taos Valley. Although Ortiz had established the grant's north line at the pueblo boundary, the settlement soon spilled onto Indian lands. Furthermore, new competition for water supplies developed, causing friction that has persisted intermittently to this day. In the fall of 1797, after only two planting seasons, the grantees petitioned Governor Chacón for rights to the *sobrantes* (surplus waters) from the Rio Pueblo and Rio Lucero, streams used by the Taos Indians from time immemorial.[44] The request suggests that the Rio Fernando had already proved inadequate for the settlers' needs. Obtaining a sobrante right meant that the newcomers could use any water remaining after Pueblo Indian farmers had satisfied their requirements. Chacón acceded to the petition without comment.

As these cases illustrate, subsistence farmers on the frontier maneuvered effectively to assure themselves an adequate water supply. In the first instance, long-time residents used the grant process to prevent intrusion by outsiders. On the Fernando grant, settlers managed to supplement their own meager stream by obtaining a conditional right to extra water, with the hope that it might be expanded later.

After the turn of the century, as New Mexicans spread out in a continuing search for new lands, another band of pioneers came up with their own solution to the same problem, one involving both engineering skill and an enormous amount of labor. In 1815, a surge of population growth at Taos led to establishment of several new communities north and west of the pueblo and Don Fernando plaza. At two of these, Arroyo Hondo and San Cristóbal, settlers received grants from Governor Alberto Máynez in the time-honored fashion, but title to lands at Arroyo Seco and its satellite, Desmontes, developed from a more devious pattern—one that can here only be summarized.

The history of Arroyo Seco and Desmontes began in 1745 when Governor Joaquín Codallos y Rabal made a large land grant located on the broad plain that extends south of Arroyo Hondo toward the Rio Lucero. The grantee, Antonio Martín, was the reprobate son of a famous Indian campaigner, Sebastián Martín, who also owned lands at Taos and large holdings north of Santa Cruz. The younger Martín failing to occupy the Taos property, no activity took place on the grant until early in the nineteenth century when Antonio's grandnephews, Joaquín, José, Francisco, and Mariano Sanches asserted ownership. Although documentation is lacking, their title seems to have been based on the 1745 grant to Tío Antonio, a claim disputed by other heirs. In 1816, after much legal maneuvering, the Taos alcalde divided the lands into two segments bisected by Arroyo Seco Creek. One group of Martín's heirs, represented by Miguel Tenorio of Abiquiú, sold the portion lying south and east of the stream to the Taos Indians. Subsequently known as the Tenorio Tract, that property brought extensive litigation among various claimants for the next 120 years. The other piece, between Arroyo Seco and Arroyo Hondo, came under control of Mariano Sanches, who proved to be an aggressive land developer.[45]

Although his relatives from Abiquiú contented themselves with a quick sale, don Mariano had other plans. He began a vigorous program to colonize the brush-covered flats above the Rio Hondo, becoming the founding father of Arroyo Seco and Desmontes. Unlike most men of property in colonial New Mexico, Sanches hoped to use the techniques of private enterprise to establish a new community that would enhance the value of his own lands. To assist his promotion, he sought out a kinsman, Felipe Gonzales, recognized him as a nephew, and gave him 1,250 varas of land for services past and future. In turn, the two entrepreneurs offered other potential farm sites to workmen (*trabajantes*) enlisted to clear (*desmontar*) the plain's thick growth of sage, piñón, and juniper.[46] Following customary procedure, the newcomers laid out Arroyo Seco plaza on the north bank of the little creek. Named by the brushcutters, Desmontes grew up as a scattered settlement to the north and west along the bluff overlooking the Hondo Valley. Not surprisingly, Arroyo Seco provided only a bare minimum of water for irrigation, causing the trabajantes to cooperate in construction of two major canals to supply their newly opened fields. Each one represented a formidable project; both are still in use.

To take advantage of the Lucero, gangs of laborers dug the Acequia Madre del Rio Lucero del Arroyo Seco, which runs for more than a mile across the Tenorio Tract to Arroyo Seco Creek. From that junction, water follows the channel downstream for later diversion, or is carried across the creek through a flume to a network of subsidiary ditches that total several miles in length. Since its inception, the system has serviced grain and hay fields north of Arroyo Seco plaza, as well as gardens and orchards close to the village.

In building the main canal from the Rio Hondo, La Acequia de la Cuchilla,

Sanches, Gonzales, and their followers faced an even more laborious task. From its source above present Valdez, the Cuchilla climbs up the south wall of Hondo Canyon more than two miles before reaching the plain at the top, where it divides into several laterals that water fields at Desmontes. Building the ditch, which seems to run uphill, required all the ingenuity and manpower the settlers could muster. The accomplishment is still regarded with awe by professional engineers.[47] Inevitably, Arroyo Seco's claims to water from the two rivers caused sharp disputes with Arroyo Hondo, Taos Pueblo, and Fernando de Taos. Judicial decisions have brought temporary solutions, but a final compromise, satisfactory to all, has proved difficult to achieve, as we shall see.

Why did Sanches, Gonzales, and their *compadres* willingly devote so much back-breaking toil to establish a community? In retrospect, their commitment is hard to explain; other locations nearby could have been developed much more easily. Even today, residents of Valdez, a village enjoying easy access to the Rio Hondo, cannot believe, despite solid evidence to the contrary, that their plaza was not settled until after Arroyo Seco and Desmontes. Whatever their reasons, Arroyo Seco's first settlers found what they wanted on the waterless plain above the Hondo.

In many ways, their situation exemplifies the struggle faced by all New Mexicans attempting to make homes on the frontier during the colonial era. Because they had few occupational alternatives to farming and stock raising, the settlers knew that no community could exist without an assured water supply. As we have seen, provincial officials recognized the same fact and made their decisions accordingly. Beginning with Oñate at San Juan, all New Mexico governors had to accommodate land policy to the availability of water in a semi-arid environment. Accelerating population growth caused increased competition among Hispanos and Pueblo Indians for water. Throughout New Mexico's long history, administration of that vital resource proved to be a difficult problem—a subject considered in detail in subsequent chapters.

# 2 | Water Administration During the Colonial Era

THROUGHOUT THE COLONIAL era in New Mexico, the provincial governor held ultimate authority in the administration of justice. Appointed directly by the king, governors were selected primarily for their military capabilities and seldom received formal legal training. Although they sometimes had access to printed codifications of Spanish laws, governors more often relied on custom and common sense to determine judicial decisions. In subordinate jurisdictions, provincial executives appointed prominent citizens as *alcaldes mayores*, who were empowered to settle everyday problems within their localities. Theoretically, no citizen resided more than a day's horseback ride from an alcalde, making the system reasonably accessible. More difficult issues came before the governor, either through referral from the alcaldes or on appeal by the litigants. Before Mexican independence in 1821, water matters were disposed of under this two-tiered arrangement along with other lawsuits, both civil and criminal. Alcaldes usually heard original complaints concerning inequitable apportionment, acequia damage, or right-of-way location, but petitioners could, if they chose, go straight to the governor. The latter relied on his appointees to conduct investigations and manage routine legal procedures.[1]

In addition to litigation, governors and alcaldes also reviewed petitions from settlers requesting supplementary water supplies. As we have seen, colonial authorities insisted on access to dependable water as a prerequisite for the approval of land grants in New Mexico. Scholars engaged in the history of the use of water generally agree that grants to farmland carried an implied right to irrigation water even when not specifically indicated.[2] After first occupation, however, grantees sometimes found the original source inadequate for their needs and requested some augmentation. As indicated in chapter 1, settlers on the Fernando de Taos grant discovered in 1797 after eighteen months of occupancy that the Rio Fernando failed to provide sufficient flow to irrigate their farmlands. As an improvement, they asked Governor Fernando Chacón to allow them use of the *aguas sobrantes* (surplus waters) from the Rio Pueblo and Rio Lucero. The petition was necessary because the pueblo of Taos and the Hispano community of Los Estiércoles (today's El Prado) already held recognized rights in the two streams. After due consideration, Chacón agreed to the request and ordered Taos alcalde, don Antonio Ortiz, to prepare a document indicating his decision.[3] Thus, the settlers' proposal merited a ruling by the governor, who called on his alcalde to handle the details.

Sometimes the process functioned less smoothly. In the summer of 1715, a quarrel erupted at Santa Fe over rights to a spring situated in a marsh east of the town's plaza near the parochial church. Known as La Ciénega, the area had been used by the citizenry for generations to cut hay and pasture saddle stock. As water declined in the Rio de Santa Fe during the July heat, Captain Diego Arias de Quiros, a prominent landowner, diverted the spring's flow into a storage pond he had constructed for irrigation. Not surprisingly, the captain's project evoked a loud protest from the Santa Fe *cabildo* (municipal council), which regarded the ciénega as part of the town's commons (*propios*). Asserting that the diversion dried up the marsh and caused great damage to the community, the cabildo ordered Arias to close his pond on July 23. Undaunted, the captain appealed to Governor Juan Ignacio Flores Mogollón for relief. Despite several requests to Tomás Jirón de Tejeda, the villa's *repartidor de aguas*, Arias had been unable to obtain enough water for his crops. To solve the problem, he asked Flores to grant him title to the spring, an entirely reasonable request, he said, since the ciénega remained unappropriated crown land.[4]

In response, Flores asked the cabildo to explain its actions and present documents establishing community ownership of the ciénega. When council members admitted that they had no papers, the governor named a four-man commission to inspect the area and advise him as to possible changes caused by the pond. After a careful examination, the commission reported that altering the spring's natural course would lower the water table and diminish forage produced in the marsh. Nevertheless, the governor largely ignored their recommendations. In an attempt at compromise, he conceded most of the ciénega to the villa as commons, but he also granted Arias rights to the spring, with an important proviso: declaring loftily that the community must not suffer from advancement of an individual, Flores ruled that, if at the end of one year diversion of the spring caused deterioration in the marsh, the grant would be voided and the pond closed.

The settlement soon fell apart. In December 1715, Captain Félix Martínez, former commanding officer of the Santa Fe presidio, became acting governor. A cabildo member when the water dispute began, Martínez was also a bitter enemy of his predecessor, Flores Mogollón. Bad blood had arisen between them after Flores informed the viceroy of certain irregularities in supply contracts at the presidio during Martínez's tour as commandant.[5] With one of their own holding office as chief executive, the councilors lost no time in petitioning for revocation of the *merced de agua* made to Arias, which, they implied, had been expedited by friendship between grantor and grantee. Noting that the one-year trial had expired, the cabildo declared that since the reconquest, *zacate* growth in the ciénega had never been so short. The members begged Martínez to recognize his predecessor's promise of preference for the community by restoring the status quo ante. After consultation with the same four experts, who again disparaged the ciénega's condition, Martínez cancelled the grant on August 11, 1716 and ordered Arias to fill in his pond.[6]

### Characteristics of the Colonial Judicial Process

The foregoing controversy illustrates several important aspects of colonial water policy. Like the petition from the Taos settlers, it demonstrates the procedure by which provincial officials authorized grants of water to deserving citizens. The case also shows a genuine concern for community welfare—a policy goal that recurs frequently in water litigation from that era. Although ultimately unsuccessful, Flores's attempt to attain consensus through a compromise in which the contending parties each receive something is characteristic of the colonial judicial process. Finally, an element of personal animosity pervades the proceedings that is difficult to evaluate. Was the case decided on its merits, or was it simply a small part of the lengthy struggle for economic and political power between Martínez and Flores Mogollón? Some of the same elements reappear in a subsequent dispute that concerned enforcement of local water regulations imposed during a time of scarcity.

In mid-July 1722, drought again withered crops along the Rio de Santa Fe. Recognizing that unregulated water use would be disastrous for the citizenry, don Francisco Bueno de Bohorques y Corcuera, Santa Fe's alcalde mayor, initiated measures that would minimize discord and inconvenience. To promote good government, (*buen gobierno*) within the villa, Bueno appointed two *juezes repartidores,* one for each side of the river, who inspected farmlands and acequias in their respective jurisdictions and allocated water to the owners on the basis of need. Certain restrictions applied. Those who failed to cultivate or carefully weed their fields faced a water embargo. Favoritism toward relatives or compadres was strictly forbidden. Thus, the alcalde hoped to regulate the distribution process and ensure that widows and other *pobres* received enough water for their small fields and gardens. Once appointed, the two juezes were entitled to the same deference and respect due the alcalde himself; miscreants faced a fine of twenty-five pesos and eight days in jail. To supervise the barrio de Analco south of the river, Bueno named Captain Nicolás Ortiz, a soldier who had distinguished himself during the Reconquest and in later campaigns against the Utes. For the area near the plaza on the north bank, the alcalde appointed Tomás Jirón Tejeda, who had previously held the same office, as mentioned earlier.[7] Both men came to New Mexico in 1694 with the colonists recruited in Mexico City.

Curiously, within a year, Ortiz himself fell afoul of the alcalde's regulations after the captain had left office. Following the admonition to help the poor, Jirón de Tejeda had permitted Cristóbal de Armenta, an impecunious youth of twenty who was responsible for the support of an aging mother, to make use of the acequia on a Sunday night in July 1723. Armenta shared his turn with several other *pobres* who worked their small fields together with him. During the night, as he spread the acequia's flow over the *milpas,* at some point Armenta found that he had no more water. At daylight on Monday, he trudged upstream to investigate and found that Captain Ortiz had turned the acequia into his wheat field. After lodging a complaint with Bueno de Bohorques, Armenta returned to the Ortiz rancho accompanied by Jirón and another repartidor. When asked for an explanation, the captain first claimed that he was merely taking advantage of an unexpected overflow, but once the two repartidors found the acequia blocked with chunks of sod (*céspedes*), a confrontation resulted. As tempers rose, Ortiz called Armenta a lying dog and attempted to strike him with his hoe, but Jirón intervened and ordered the aggressor to present himself before Bueno de Bohorques without delay.

Despite Jirón's order, sundown came before the meeting took place, in the doorway of the presidial guardhouse. The ensuing interview did not go well. After rejecting the captain's account of the irrigation incident, Bueno de Bohorques demanded an explanation for his belated arrival. Ortiz insolently replied that the midday sun made him ill, to which the alcalde answered that ample shade could be found in the guardhouse, calling on the corporal on duty to make an arrest. Defiantly, the captain drew his sword and ran across the plaza, outdistancing the corporal and two soldiers, as he gained asylum in the parish church. With Ortiz safely established inside the church, Bueno de Bohorques launched an extensive investigation of the entire affair, collecting depositions from all the participants. He then drew up a four-count indictment and demanded that Ortiz leave his sanctuary to face trial. The captain had other plans, however. Hoping for support, he appealed to his old comrade-in-arms, Lieutenant General Juan Páez Hurtado, a veteran of the reconquest, then serving as lieutenant governor of New Mexico. In a lengthy petition, Ortiz repeated his version of the confrontation and asked that the alcalde recuse himself from the case, claiming that his irascible temper made a fair hearing impossible. He also asserted that his enforced confinement had caused substantial losses to his crops and livestock from lack of supervision.

Somewhat sympathetic, Páez Hurtado had the alcalde's hefty case file delivered to him for an official review. Observing that no verdict had been rendered, he ordered a delay in the proceedings until Governor Juan Domingo de Bustamante returned to the capital, thus removing the issue from the jurisdiction of Bueno de Bohorques. Páez also allowed Ortiz to leave his ecclesiastical refuge without fear of arrest until summoned by the governor.[8] Final disposition of the case is unrecorded, but it seems unlikely that the captain suffered a severe penalty in view of his status and past military record. Although the case manifests petty politics and personal animosities, it also demonstrates continuing official concern for community welfare. Through his regulations, Bueno de Bohorques attempted to allocate the villa's water resources equitably and showed sincere concern for less fortunate citizens. By threatening significant fines and imprisonment for unauthorized water use or disrespect toward the appointed juezes, he meant to assure compliance by truculent citizens. Finally, it should be noted that the juezes repartidores of that era undertook many of the responsibilities later assumed by mayordomos of various acequias. In this instance, however, the officers represented an entire community rather than groups of landowners using a particular ditch.

*Compromises*

Frequently, New Mexico's officials managed to apportion water resources among competing parties without the rancor that characterized the confrontation with Nicolás Ortiz. In the Tesuque Valley north of Santa Fe, for example, rivalry for irrigation water intensified during the colonial period as settlement increased, but the contending factions usually contrived a satisfactory compromise, with help from governmental authorities. Such an agreement resulted from a land grant awarded in 1752 to Juan de Gabaldón at the upper end of the valley, where the Rio Tesuque bursts out of the Sangre de Cristo Mountains. In his request to Governor Tomás Vélez Cachupín, Gabaldón stated that scarcity of water in the capital city had prevented him from finding a suitable location there to support his large family. As usual, Vélez ordered the villa's alcalde mayor, José de Bustamante Tagle, to confer with Tesuque Pueblo leaders and other interested parties as to possible adverse claims. Immediately, Corporal Juan de Benavides, owner of a substantial tract downstream, protested that "not a drop of water" would reach his rancho if settlement took place at the canyon. In reply, Bustamante observed that water was already so scarce that, even without additional use, the corporal was unlikely to receive enough to supply his fields. To improve the situation, Gabaldón promised to lead a cooperative effort for construction of a reservoir that would capture spring runoff for the benefit of the entire community. Accordingly, Vélez approved the grant and Bustamante placed the applicant in possession with a final warning not to impede his neighbors' water supply.[9]

Despite the promise of storage offered by Gabaldón's *tanque,* succeeding governors occasionally found it necessary to adjust the allocation schedule between Hispano settlers and their Pueblo Indian neighbors. During litigation circa 1770, Governor Pedro Fermín de Mendinueta authorized the Benavides family to take whatever water they needed for twenty-four hours every eight days, with the pueblo retaining exclusive use at other times. Several years later, Mendinueta's successor, Juan Bautista de Anza, increased the settlers' share significantly by allowing them use of a single small acequia at their discretion.

In 1788, when the heirs and successors of Juan de Benavides requested help in determining land titles and water rights at Tesuque, Governor Fernando de la Concha sent Alcalde Antonio José Ortiz out to the valley to make an investigation. After reviewing the rulings handed down by previous governors, Ortiz set up a weekly schedule that curtailed Hispano use to the period from daylight Monday to sundown Tuesday.[10] Clearly, in this region of limited resources, apportionment was subject to change when necessary, but the procedure seems to have been fair to all parties. In 1776, during his famous inspection of New Mexico's Franciscan missions, Fray Francisco Atanasio Domínguez described the Hispano settlement at Tesuque as "a little valley which hangs from the sierra . . . sprinkled with ranchos. . . . They are watered by a very scanty river of good water. . . . The crops are very good and sufficient." Fray Francisco also admired the fields adjoining the pueblo. "All are under irrigation," he wrote, "for although the river is short . . . the Indians are long on ingenuity. The land . . . usually yields a good deal of grain of all kinds sown there."[11]

If settlers at Tesuque sometimes interfered with the pueblo's water supply, the Indians were guilty of similar offenses against their neighbors downstream at Cuyamungué. In 1805, a group of anxious farmers headed by José Julián Quintana complained to Pojoaque's alcalde, Manuel Delgado, that the Tesuques had begun construction of a new ditch, threatening to divert the flow from a certain spring on which they depended. When the Indians ignored Delgado's order to cease and desist, the plaintiffs turned to Governor Joaquín del Real Alencaster for help. After an inspection by a subordinate, Alencaster ruled that the new acequia caused no injury of itself, but warned the pueblo not to interfere with the rancheros' rights.

The governor's decision resolved the issue for almost forty years, but it was reopened in June 1842 in the midst of the irrigation season. Representatives from Cuyamungué appeared before Diego Archuleta, prefect of New Mexico's northern district, protesting that, once again, the Tesuques had seized the springs above them. To irrigate some newly plowed fields, the Indians had diverted water from the springs into tanks, thus causing great injury to the parched fields below. While conceding that the springs originated on Tesuque lands, the farmers claimed a right to them through many years of use. They reminded the prefect of Alencaster's earlier decree. Archuleta turned the case over to a Santa Fe alcalde, who gathered representatives from both sides before him for arbitration. After much discussion, they hammered out a compromise that reallocated the water supply in an equitable manner, agreeable to all. The signers agreed that the compact was binding forever, in both wet and dry years. Once again, the opposed parties had proved capable of working out a settlement, with some prodding by concerned officials. Like similar water agreements from the Spanish and Mexican periods, many years later it was recorded by the county clerk, which suggests it remained in force.[12]

In addition to water theft, the issue of acequia right-of-way sometimes caused friction among neighbors. Although conveyance of water across another's property may result in losses or inconvenience, the right to do so is a fundamental part of irrigation law. Suits for damages caused by acequias occurred frequently in New Mexico, as we shall see. A case of that kind originated at Albuquerque in January 1733 when Cristóbal García began construction of a new ditch from the Rio del Norte. Three adjoining landowners, Isabel Jorge, Felipe Gallegos, and Antonio Gurulé, directed a complaint to Alcalde Juan Gonzales Bas in which they claimed that the proposed acequia ran too close to their houses and prevented their livestock from using an accustomed watering place. Furthermore, the project was not needed because García already had free access to a ditch belonging to Captain Juan Griego, an arrangement that had allowed him to gather abundant harvests in the past. As a matter of justice, the plaintiffs asked for an injunction barring further use of the new acequia. García responded quickly, noting that he had already received permission from the governor to take the ditch across his neighbors' lands, which were largely uncultivated. He conceded that Griego had graciously allowed use of his acequia, but asserted that it lacked sufficient capacity to water all the fields under it. Sandy soil made further enlargement impossible. Because he supported a household of nineteen, he badly needed the big crops harvested recently: the crops, he said, had come about through constant toil from sunup to sundown by the entire family.[13]

Once the lawsuit had been joined, the litigants bombarded Gonzales with additional charges and countercharges. At one point, the plaintiffs attempted some legal trickery, claiming a conflict of interest by the alcalde. In a petition to Governor Gervasio Cruzat y Góngora, they asked that Gonzales withdraw from the case because he favored their opponent; his secretary, Isidro Sánchez, they said, had drawn up various writs in García's support. Unimpressed, the governor ordered Gonzales to complete his investigation, but reserved final determination of the outcome to himself. As the vituperation increased, the contending parties appeared to be deadlocked, but suddenly, after a month of wrangling, they reached a compromise. Piously recalling an admonition in the holy gospel urging Christians to preserve the peace, the litigants proposed an agreement intended to settle the dispute and restore communal well-being. Under its terms, García gave up his ditch, but in return, received authorization to rehabilitate an abandoned acequia formerly used by Gurulé that served the lands in question. The beneficiary also assumed responsibility for any damage to the ditch caused by livestock grazing in the vicinity. Finally, all parties agreed that neither they nor their successors could ever reopen the suit, a common provision in colonial legal documents. Not surprisingly, the settlement received immediate approval from both the alcalde and the governor, with the stipulation that Gonzales Bas receive twenty-four pesos compensation for time and trouble expended on the case.[14] Once again, as in cases cited previously, litigants and officials managed to arrange a satisfactory settlement in keeping with popular values.

A similar suit began at Abiquiú in the spring of 1815 when the Rio Chama roared down the valley, overflowing its banks and devastating crop lands along the way. One victim of the river's wrath, Alférez Mariano Martínez, blamed his considerable loss of topsoil on an acequia crossing his property that had been built by Manuel Martínez, a neighbor and relative. After Mariano filed a formal complaint to force closure of Manuel's ditch, local authorities sent a three-man delegation under the leadership of Francisco Salazar to examine the site and recommend appropriate action, a traditional procedure in water disputes. The inspectors quickly decided that Mariano's losses had resulted from topographical conditions at the location, not from Manuel's irrigation system. To solve the quarrel, Salazar gathered the principals and their legal representatives at his house, but a long discussion failed to bring an agreement. Disgusted, the arbitrator sought direction from Governor Alberto Máynez, who appointed a powerful Santa Fe politico, Juan Rafael Ortiz, as a special judge empowered to go to Abiquiú and end the dispute. Although unrecorded, Ortiz's decision apparently favored Mariano Martínez, who, in testimony presented during a similar lawsuit in 1832, was reported to be the judge's good friend.[15] In the 1832 case, influence in high places seems to have outweighed local consensus in determining the outcome. Decisions of that type were the exception rather than the rule, however.

In some locations, engineering problems made the allocation process very difficult. A situation of that kind came about near the end of the colonial era at the village of La Puebla in the Santa Cruz Valley. On May 12, 1819, Governor Facundo Melgares received a complaint from Diego Antonio Martín, a local farmer, charging that overflow from the community acequia damaged his crop lands. Because earlier appeals to the alcalde mayor of Santa Cruz, Matías Ortiz, had gone unanswered, Martín requested that the governor appoint an impartial mediator to resolve the matter. Reluctant to bypass his bureaucracy, Melgares asked Ortiz for an explanation. The alcalde's report revealed that, some years earlier, Martín and the acequia's other *parciantes* (water users) had attempted to improve their irrigation system by relocating the ditch. Martín, who had subsequently purchased land crossed by the new channel, refused to cooperate in shoring up the ditch banks to curtail flooding. Stubbornly, he had rejected a cash settlement of twenty-five pesos suggested by Ortiz, although he continued to claim substantial crop loss.

When Melgares called on Martín for more information, the latter responded with a lengthy discourse replete with references to the needs of his large family and aged mother, much as Cristóbal García had done many years before. He also accused Ortiz of acting as both judge and counsel for his opponents, an obvious conflict of interest. To resolve the problem, he suggested that the acequia be returned to its old channel. Puzzled by the conflicting testimony, the governor sent an alcalde from Santa Fe to make an investigation and offer some advice, as Martín had requested in his first petition. Arriving at the site, the governor's representative gathered the ditch owners and soon discovered that they had no documents allowing the change of right-of-way, a serious shortcoming. During his inspection, he found the acequia's overflow at a large barranca, a topographical feature that the parciantes had struggled to cross without success. As a solution, he offered two alternatives: use the intake of the new ditch to bring water on the barranca's lower side, or reactivate the old channel. Without much hesitation, Melgares approved the second procedure in an order dated May 26, 1819.[16]

Evidently, the governor's decree failed to end right-of-way problems between Diego Antonio Martín and his neighbors. Nine years later, on May 28, 1828, the ditch owners gathered at the *sala consistorial* (courtroom) in Santa Cruz to draw up a written agreement determining future management practices—a very unusual procedure at that time. As a demonstration of unity, the parciantes vowed to continue maintaining the acequia together as a group. To safeguard Martín's fields, the other owners promised to provide materials needed to prevent future flooding, noting that they had already hauled in nine cartloads of limbs and branches (*ramos*). They also recognized that Martín's responsibility for cleaning the ditch did not extend beyond his own lands. Duly signed by all concerned, the document was then validated by the villa's alcalde, as requested by the signatories. Significantly, the agreement received a second validation thirty years later. On April 8, 1858, Elias T. Clark, clerk of Rio Arriba County Probate Court, recorded the same document in the county records, suggesting that successors to Martín and his associates continued to face many of the same difficulties in looking after their ditch.[17]

A comparable situation arose at Taos in 1817, when a group of vecinos (citizens) from the Don Fernando grant headed by José Martín appeared before Alcalde Tomás Ortiz to protest destruction caused by a poorly located millrace. Briefly reviewing the grant's history, Martín, the community mayordomo, recalled that after receiving possession of their lands, the settlers constructed ditches on each side of the Rio Fernando, now known as the Acequia del Sur and the Acequia del Norte del Cañon. The second of these terminated in the Acequia Madre del Rio Pueblo, the ditch carrying the sobrante unused by the Taos Indians and awarded to the settlers in 1797. According to Martín, the system provided equitable distribution satisfactory to all. Major difficulties occurred, however, when excess water from a mill operated by Vicente Trujillo washed out the northside ditch and flooded both the road to the farmlands and the public highway following the river. Attempts at making repairs had caused considerable losses of time and resources needed elsewhere. In his response,

Alcalde Ortiz emphasized that the public welfare (*bien común*) must be the over-
riding consideration in such situations. He decreed that, if investigation proved
the allegations to be true, Trujillo's mill and millrace must be altered or eliminated.[18]

*Flood Control: Controversies and Cooperation*

Attempts at flood control along New Mexico's major streams also led to
controversies from time to time. Excessive runoff often caused serious problems,
particularly in the spring when heavy mountain snowpack began to melt. A
squabble of that kind broke out at Abiquiú on the Rio Chama in 1746 after
Miguel Martín Serrano complained of efforts by the Valdés family to prevent
the river's relentless erosion of their fields. Hispano settlement in the area began
in 1734, when ten families received allotments of farmlands extending up the
Chama from its confluence with El Rito to the prehistoric pueblo of Abiquiú,
about six miles upstream. During the possession ceremony, conducted by Lieutenant General Juan Páez Hurtado, on September 1, Martín Serrano received
1.25 fanegas of bottomland well-suited for irrigation on the river's south bank.[19]
As the settlement began to put down roots, its citizens received a license in 1737
from don Martín Elizacoechea, the bishop of Durango in New Spain, to erect a
chapel near Martín's rancho. Subsequently, the neighborhood became known as
La Capilla. In 1739, several members of the Valdés family, Rosa, Ignacio, and
Juan Lorenzo, received a land grant north of the river across from Martín.[20]

Discovering after a few years in residence that the Chama frequently inundated part of their fields, the Valdeses erected a levee (*estacada*) in 1746 to keep
the monster at bay. Situated across the stream, Martín feared that the Valdés
barrier would send the river raging through his property and sweep away the
new chapel, which lacked only a roof for its completion. In a petition to Governor Joaquín Codallos y Rabal, he demanded a halt to further construction, observing that the original settlers had shunned the Valdés location because of the
obvious flood danger. Following customary procedure, the governor called for
an investigation, to be made by Juan de Beytia, lieutenant alcalde of Santa Cruz.
After riding over to Abiquiú, Beytia found that, although the river bed between
the two ranchos had widened to an alarming fifty-two varas, the levee served
to keep the Chama in its normal channel and threatened no property damage
whatever. The complaint, he declared, was entirely frivolous. Disgusted by
these revelations, Codallos ordered Martín Serrano to disturb his neighbors no
more, threatening a hefty fine of fifty pesos for further false claims.[21] Ironically,
Martín's prediction of serious erosion came true in later years, as the Chama
gradually chewed its way south, cutting into Abiquiú's historic plaza, although
it never reached the ruins of the old chapel, which still remain.[22]

Although flood damage sometimes caused disagreements, it also brought
about interesting attempts at cooperation, in which different communities

would agree to share an acequia for a period of time. Like water apportionment, arrangements of that kind had to be carefully negotiated and approved by proper authorities. In 1770, spring flooding again ravaged the Abiquiú vicinity, carrying off the diversion dam and intake that served La Capilla. Instead of rebuilding, the parciantes obtained permission to use the principal ditch belonging to the *genízaro* (detribalized Indians living among the Spaniards) pueblo of Santo Tomás de Abiquiú, founded by Governor Vélez Cachupín in 1754. In return, the settlers provided a proportionate part of the labor, tools, and materials required for annual maintenance. The arrangement functioned well enough for almost thirty years, until 1797, when Governor Fernando Chacón issued a decree which granted an absolute priority in the joint-use ditch to the genízaros, probably at their request. Wistfully, the citizens of La Capilla, under the leadership of Juan and Severino Martín, asked Chacón for permission to re-open their old headgates if he insisted on terminating the earlier accord. Reiterating his previous edict, the governor authorized the changeover, with the usual stipulation that no injury occur to a third party.[23]

Almost ten years later, residents of Los Silvestres, a tiny village west of Abiquiú, negotiated a deal to share the community's acequia madre. Located at the mouth of the rocky gorge where the Chama Valley widens sufficiently for cultivation, Los Silvestres had little land to spare for ditch rights-of-way, a condition aggravated occasionally by floods. On August 30, 1806, José Manuel Velarde, Pedro Trujillo, and Santiago Salazar appeared before Juan Antonio Barela, political and military lieutenant for the jurisdiction, to certify a contract that they had drawn up. Under its terms, Velarde, who had purchased all rights to the area's oldest acequia, allowed certain farmers represented by Trujillo and Salazar to irrigate fields they had planted under his ditch. The agreement was necessary because the petitioners had no ditch of their own and no place to put one. To become parciantes, the group promised to assist in cleaning the entire acequia each year and to deny its use to anyone guilty of stealing water. An unusual clause stipulated that two mayordomos would share responsibility for management—one for the acequia's full length and one for the lower portion. The latter had superior powers, however, suggesting that Velarde's lands lay toward the further end. Other landholders might join later by paying reasonable compensation for the privilege.[24] In addition to demonstrating a typical pragmatic solution to a potentially troublesome problem, this document is also interesting as one of the first written references to the title *mayordomo* as a local official responsible for acequia administration.

As illustrated by the previous examples, New Mexican authorities usually managed to settle water questions through regular governmental procedures without great difficulty. Sometimes, however, emotions rose to such a pitch that the parties resorted to violence, as in the case in which Nicolás Ortiz rudely appropriated his neighbors' irrigation water without official approval. Almost invariably, conflict resulted from a single cause: sudden seizure of an acequia's flow by an unauthorized user during a time when another party enjoyed its benefits. While the cause may have been almost always the same, the responses by colonial officials to such infractions varied widely, depending on the nature of the case.

On July 31, 1745, a confrontation between Juan Antonio Salazar and his neighbor and kinsman, Manuel Valerio, took place on the lower Chama near its junction with the Rio Grande. Thirty years earlier, Salazar's father, Antonio, had received a land grant in the area and had taken out an acequia from the Chama, thus establishing a priority of use. Subsequently, Valerio had purchased lands nearby served by the same ditch. According to Salazar, trouble began when Valerio commandeered all the water for two days without permission. When Juan Antonio diverted the canal into his own fields, the offender arrived in a fury. After some name-calling, Valerio struck Salazar on the head with a shovel, making a nasty gash. From his sickbed, the victim fired off a complaint to Lieutenant Alcalde Beytia in Santa Cruz, demanding that Valerio be jailed and his few chattels be confiscated as bond until a settlement had been reached. To bolster his case, the petitioner declared that his opponent had taken the water illegally, since he, Salazar, was the recognized owner of the ditch (*dueño de dha zequia*).

After a thorough inquiry, Beytia turned his findings over to Governor Codallos, who rendered a decision intended to reconcile the two adversaries and restore harmony to the community. Ignoring Salazar's legalistic claims of ownership, he ordered Beytia to bring the parties together and persuade them to forgive each other as relatives and countrymen. In keeping with the governor's admonition, the case ended with an *abrazo* by the two combatants, and payment of eight pesos each to the alcalde for the vexation they had caused.[25]

A similar incident troubled colonial officials in 1819 at the Plaza de Nuestra Señora de Dolores within the jurisdiction of Chimayó. Tempers flared on that occasion after don Julián Quintana, the aged mayordomo of la Acequia de la Cañada Ancha, allowed a turn on the ditch to Miguel Espinosa, a small farmer of mixed blood (a *coyote*). By diverting the water into his field, Espinosa cut off another parciante, the militiaman Manuel Vigil, who had been irrigating nearby. When he discovered what had happened, Vigil vented his anger by attacking Espinosa with a shovel. The latter swung his hoe in retaliation and the two grappled, falling into the muddy acequia with a death grip on each other's hair. Espinosa clearly had the worst of it until Vigil's two sons came up and persuaded their father to depart, leaving his adversary with assorted bruises and contusions.

On orders from Governor Melgares, a local official made the obligatory investigation and found that Espinosa's injuries had put him in bed. To begin, the alcalde took a long deposition from the victim and examined his wounds, which seemed to be healing nicely. He then sought out Quintana, who confirmed that Espinosa had been entitled to use the water, adding that the militiaman was a quarrelsome fellow with little respect for community officials. The mayordomo also recalled that, after the fight, Vigil had ridden to Abiquiú to enlist the support of his commanding officer, Alférez Mariano Martín, no stranger to water fights, as we have seen.

Once returned, Vigil presented Quintana with a letter from the alférez defending his subordinate's actions. According to Martín, Vigil deserved no punishment because he, as a Spaniard and a soldier, need not consider the rights of a lowly coyote such as Espinosa. The racial slur had little influence, however. With his report completed, the alcalde marched Vigil off to Santa Fe under guard, forwarding the complete case file to the governor. When Melgares found that Espinosa's injuries were not so serious as first believed, he took a more tolerant view of Vigil's misdeeds, much as Codallos had done previously. After considering all the testimony collected, he restored the militiaman to freedom on payment of a modest ten peso fine.[26] In this instance, the transgressor escaped with only minor punishment.

A third example that began in violence near Ranchos de Taos had more serious implications. On a summer morning in 1796, Juan Ignacio Vigil noticed, as he delivered a mule to his father, that the acequia madre that served his rancho was running bank-full. Eager to irrigate some wheat, Vigil quickly returned home and had opened the ditch into his farmlands when he saw a neighbor, José Armijo, brazenly cut off the water. Although he tried to reason with the usurper, the two began to struggle and had dropped to the ground when, suddenly, Armijo died. As others hurriedly came up, inspection of the corpse revealed no wounds or other injuries to explain this shocking turn of events. Nevertheless, Vigil galloped off to Santa Fe in a panic to take sanctuary at the parish church, just as Nicolás Ortiz had done some seventy years before. On this occasion, the traditional refuge proved to be ineffective. Using a procedure known as *caución juratoria,* which allowed authorities to remove suspects from sanctuary in certain circumstances, Governor Fernando Chacón ordered Vigil taken to the presidial guardhouse, pending trial. After a spirited presentation by the defendant's legal representative, Chacón took the case under advisement, while Vigil languished in jail.[27] Fortunately, he was released after a year's confinement through a decree from the Audiencia of Guadalajara announcing a general pardon (*indulto*) that freed prisoners throughout the empire.[28]

To summarize, colonial authorities considered a variety of water issues in the course of their regular duties. At the local level, alcaldes mayores usually managed to resolve disputes within their jurisdictions, but provincial governors sometimes determined the outcome of more difficult cases. Equitable distribution of irrigation water was the issue litigated most frequently, but other problems included right-of-way location and flood control. During judicial proceedings, officials relied more on custom than abstract principles in reaching verdicts. Through their decisions, magistrates attempted to heal rifts within the community rather than determine the winners and losers of water lawsuits. On rare occasions, personal influence appears to have affected the outcome. In cases involving physical violence, authorities seldom imposed harsh sentences, even when serious crimes had been committed. However, mild punishment for criminal behavior of all kinds seems to have been the norm throughout New Spain, perhaps again reflecting community values that favored leniency for defendants.[29]

# 3 | Water Administration During the Mexican Era

N EW MEXICO'S POPULATION having grown steadily during the last decades of Spanish rule—rising almost 50 percent, from about 25,000 in 1790 to more than 36,000 in 1817—more irrigated farmland was needed for sustenance. Settlement expanded in every direction. From the Rio Pecos to Cebolleta and from Taos to Socorro, government officials authorized new land grants on the frontiers of the province. On the eve of Mexican independence, farming and stockraising remained the dominant forms of economic activity for the majority of New Mexicans.[1] Despite the great importance of agriculture for all levels of society, Spanish and Mexican documents provide few reports concerning crop production, farming techniques, or weather conditions. There is an interesting exception from the Mexican period, however. In 1840, Governor Manuel Armijo, on orders from his superiors, requested information concerning mining and agriculture in the Santa Clara region of the upper Rio Grande Valley. Filtering down through bureaucratic channels, his inquiry came to the attention of Juan Cristóbal García, a minor functionary serving as a substitute *juez de paz* (justice of the peace). García immediately claimed complete ignorance of local mineral resources, but managed to produce a useful summary of the agricultural situation within his jurisdiction that is probably accurate for much of New Mexico both before and after that time.[2]

After making a modest reference to the time and effort devoted to the report, García began with a list of the district's principal field crops, which included maize, wheat, barley, peas, lentils, and several kinds of beans. Planted in March and April, these grains and legumes matured at varying times between July and October. Once harvested, they usually sold for two pesos per fanega (1.6 bushels), although *frijol* and *garbanzo* brought a little more. García reported that most farmers marketed their crops in small quantities close to home, using carts and pack trains for transportation. He made no mention of commodity sales to other parts of Mexico.

In addition to the staples, producers also raised an assortment of fruits and vegetables: apricots, peaches, apples, plums, melons, onions, garlic, and chiles, that commanded a range of prices. They also grew *punche,* a variety of coarse tobacco important in the Indian trade, worth two reales (a real = 1/8 peso) for a handful. Turning to land tenure, García declared that farmers in his district all owned the fields they cultivated, indicating an absence of tenancy. Each year began with spring plowing, seeding, and ditch cleaning, followed by irrigation and weed control, and ended with the harvest in late summer or fall. Emphasizing the importance of irrigation water to maintain production, García observed that farmers near Santa Clara depended on the Rio del Norte and the Rio Chama to water their fields and turn their gristmills. Although treacherous during spring floods, the two rivers supplied the community's lifeblood.[3]

When Mexico won independence from Spain in 1821, the new government incorporated some changes in the local administrative structure that encouraged greater public participation. Reforms included reestablishment of popularly elected municipal councils, known sometimes as *cabildos,* sometimes as *ayuntamientos.* At Santa Fe, a cabildo had functioned almost from the villa's founding early in the seventeenth century. After the reconquest, a revived council contended for power with the governor and other officials, as noted above in the case of Diego Arias de Quiros. Around 1720, however, the institution was eliminated, which must have pleased its political opponents. No similar bodies existed elsewhere in New Mexico until after adoption of the liberal Spanish constitution of Cádiz in 1812. Several ayuntamientos then sprang up, at Santa Fe, Santa Cruz de la Cañada, and other locations, but all were suppressed within two years after the reactionary monarch, Ferdinand VII, resumed the throne. In 1820, a revolt by liberal Spanish political and military leaders forced the king to restore the Cádiz constitution, so that many New Mexico communities again boasted ayuntamientos shortly before independence. As Mexico became a sovereign state, the municipal councils relieved governors and alcaldes of some local responsibilities, including water administration.[4]

## Taos: A Useful Case Study

One of the more active and best-documented councils was located at Taos, on the far northern frontier. A consideration of attempts made by its members to resolve community water problems provides a useful case study of local government during the Mexican period. As in other settlements, the Taos ayuntamiento consisted of six *regidores* (aldermen), presided over by an *alcalde constitucional* chosen from the membership, and a *sindico procurador* (town attorney), all elected by popular vote.[5] Charged by the central government to work for the advancement of agriculture, the council regarded responsible resource administration as a primary duty. Water issues most often discussed included allocation disputes between competing settlements, questions of priority, rights-of-way, acequia maintenance, and related problems. The members also were empowered to advise the governor concerning the disposition of public lands for the creation of new settlements.

When the Taos ayuntamiento opened for business, it represented a rapidly growing community. As indicated by the preceding chapters, settlement had been reestablished after the reconquest on the Rio de las Trampas at Ranchos de Taos, and near the pueblo at Los Estiércoles (El Prado). Population growth had been slow at first, but between 1790 and 1821, the number of Hispanos in the region had quadrupled from about 300 to more than 1,200 persons. Following establishment of the Don Fernando de Taos grant in 1796, new placitas originated at the present site of Taos and at Cañón. A few leagues to the north, settlement began at Arroyo Hondo, Arroyo Seco, and Desmontes in 1815, as we have seen. Inevitably, population expansion increased competition for land and water between Hispanos and the pueblo, and also among different groups of settlers.[6] As newcomers arrived, they sometimes constructed irrigation works before their water rights had been clearly defined. From the beginning, the Taos ayuntamiento faced serious issues of resource allocation. In rendering decisions, the regidores usually adopted a conservative position favoring well-established landowners, to the great disappointment of outsiders eager for new farmlands and the water needed to maintain them.

In July 1823, for example, the ayuntamiento attempted to resolve a controversy between inhabitants of Arroyo Hondo and Desmontes concerning water from the Rio Hondo. Eight years earlier, settlers at Arroyo Hondo had received possession of an authorized grant from Governor Alberto Máynez that included extensive irrigable farmlands in the river valley. Located west of Arroyo Seco village, the Desmontes community spread out haphazardly over the brushy plain that rises abruptly from the Hondo's south bank. Although residents there claimed ownership through an older grant made to Antonio Martín in 1745, occupation had occurred only recently, clouding title to the lands. With enormous effort, people at Desmontes had excavated the Cuchilla acequia up the steep south side of the valley to water their fields above. The project caused immediate protests from Arroyo Hondo farmers, who appealed to the ayuntamiento for redress.[7] Their position was compromised by a *merced* (grant), also made in 1815, by Máynez, that allowed Felipe Gonzales and his associates at Desmontes to appropriate an unspecified quantity of water from the Rio Hondo.[8] After mulling over this thorny problem, the ayuntamiento ruled that settlers at Arroyo Hondo possessed "a total and absolute right" in the river by virtue of their land grant; other claimants must allow sufficient flow to irrigate the fields of the preferred community. The decision included a small loophole, however. By obtaining permission from their neighbors below, Desmontes farmers could use their hard-earned ditch, and that is what they did.[9] Thus, the ayuntamiento settled the dispute, but only temporarily.

Six months later, the council considered a similar complaint concerning apportionment of the Rio Lucero that aligned the village of Arroyo Seco against the pueblo of Taos and settlers downstream at Don Fernando and Los Estiércoles. Trouble had been brewing since pioneers at Arroyo Seco discovered that the meager stream bordering their lands was, as the name suggests, inadequate for irrigation. Like their neighbors at Desmontes, the settlers dug an acequia from the Rio Lucero, which descended out of the mountains more than a mile away, across the plain to the southeast. Unwisely, Arroyo Seco's leading citizens, Mariano Sanches and Felipe Gonzales, asserted extravagant claims to the Lucero, infuriating irrigators already dependent on the river's flow, and the latter objected vigorously to the ayuntamiento.

After careful deliberation, the regidores ruled that, on the basis of ancient usage, the pueblo of Taos possessed first rights in the Lucero, followed by farmers at Los Estiércoles and Don Fernando (who, as noted earlier, had claimed the river's sobrantes). Arroyo Seco was not completely shut out, however. Recalling the mandate to protect agriculture, the ayuntamiento allotted that community a single *surco* (in modern terms, an amount sufficient to fill a twelve-inch pipe) so that planting there would not be lost. Thus, the council arranged a compromise that recognized priority of use but also acknowledged the needs of later applicants; no petitioner received all he asked, but no one was left empty-handed. Frequently cited by historians and attorneys involved in water rights litigation, the ayuntamiento's ruling has become widely regarded as a judicial landmark.[10]

Despite its later acclaim, the decision failed to provide a satisfactory allocation of the Lucero's waters. When the conflict flared again some years later, the Pueblos placed a cartwheel at the ditch mouth to measure the surco allotted to Arroyo Seco, having ascertained that the aperture at the hub would meter the correct amount. Predictably, the villagers found such restraint intolerable; government officials ignored the situation.

About 1838, serious conflict threatened between the pueblo and Los Estiércoles, on one side, and Arroyo Seco, on the other. According to testimony presented by José Rafael Gallegos of Los Estiércoles in 1890, during later litigation, the two factions agreed on a date for a confrontation and marched up to the intake, armed and ready for battle. Before shots were fired, however, a tremendous cloudburst forced the belligerants to seek cover. After the skies cleared, the combatants saw that the Lucero had flooded, making the issue moot. Subsequently, the cartwheel was removed and the river provided enough water to dampen the controversy for several decades.[11] Although this incident is surrounded by an almost mythical quality, it clearly demonstrates the emotional intensity generated by serious water disputes.

On another occasion, in 1825, the Taos ayuntamiento again attempted to balance the needs of old settlers and new arrivals while reviewing a petition from thirty-six families for lands within the Arroyo Hondo grant. Located at La Talaya, a high shelf north of the river, the tract had previously been occupied by others who had departed. In making their request, the petitioners specifically mentioned the abundance of water still available for irrigation from the Hondo. With approval from the council, Alcalde Severino Martínez gathered the household heads at the site on August 25, 1825, to conduct the traditional act of possession, acting in name of the Mexican congress, not Spain's king, to reflect the change in sovereignty. After he had marked off individual parcels of fifty or one hundred varas, Martínez drew up a document that gave the grantees full rights as citizens of the community, "but without prejudice to the first settlers of Arroyo Hondo who depend on its water."[12] By recognizing the legitimate claims of both groups, the ayuntamiento intended to ensure equitable apportionment of the river's resources and eliminate the potential for strife.

By the 1830s, despite continued population growth, the ayuntamiento began to adopt increasingly restrictive land and water policies. These measures were entirely in accord with the desires of their constituents: when mutual interests seemed threatened, groups of water users could abandon their usual antagonism to confront a common enemy. In 1836, for example, leaders from the pueblo of Taos allied themselves with citizens of Los Estiércoles and Don Fernando to protest a claim advanced by outsiders for lands along the Rio Lucero. Although they lacked supporting documentation, the claimants, José Vitorino Montes Vigil of El Paso and some of his kinsmen attempted to reestablish title to a grant made to, but never taken possession of, by Pedro Vigil de Santillanes in 1742. Representatives of the three allied groups petitioned the ayuntamiento, asserting that additional settlement would bring grave injury to more than four hundred families who depended on the Lucero for irrigation water. Any diminution of the river's flow could cause abandonment of existing communities. Headed by Padre Antonio José Martínez, the famed nationalist priest, signers included a host of prominent persons. Although the number of families seems inflated, the threat was real enough. Because the Vigils failed to prove themselves descendants of the original grantee and could not produce a valid title, their claim was rejected after lengthy litigation. In recommending denial by the governor, ayuntamiento members reemphasized daily use of the Lucero's water "from time immemorial" by the pueblo, Los Estiércoles, and Don Fernando.[13]

A similar situation arose a short time later in the canyon above Ranchos de Taos. On March 13, 1837, eleven landless families led by Nicolás Sandoval asked Governor Albino Pérez for a land grant at the junction of the Rio Grande del Rancho and the Rito de la Olla. In his petition, Sandoval stated that an unfriendly alcalde had dispossessed him of lands at Desmontes that he had earned as one of the laborers recruited to dig the Cuchilla acequia. Anticipating opposition from water users downstream, Sandoval offered to irrigate with springs far back in the mountains that never reached the river. As requested by the governor, the Taos ayuntamiento took charge of the customary investigation, naming a committee composed of Juan Manuel Lucero, José Jesús Trujillo, and Dr.

David Waldo, a Santa Fe trader residing in the valley. After some research, the committee reported adversely, mainly because the requested lands lay within the Rio Grande del Rancho grant made in 1795. The ayuntamiento then recommended disapproval by the governor, adding that the canyon springs mentioned by Sandoval were inadequate for irrigation and that further diversion from the river would harm three hundred families downstream.[14] In both cases, irrigators presented a united front and convinced their representatives to prevent overappropriation.

### Santa Fe: Rights-of-Way

In Santa Fe, New Mexico's capital and largest community, the ayuntamiento provided oversight for the daily management of the town's acequias. At a meeting in the spring of 1829, council members debated the qualifications needed for a repartidor de aguas—the official responsible for apportionment of irrigation water in the villa, as mentioned in chapter 2. Maintenance of the acequia system was also a serious problem. During religious holidays such as Holy Week and Corpus Christi, waste water from irrigated fields often flooded the villa's streets, forcing religious processions to make wide detours. After some discussion, the ayuntamiento decided that the repartidor must be a man of great integrity, not susceptible to bribery, capable of performing his duties with fairness to all. The proposed salary was not large: a quartilla of corn or wheat annually from each parciante, with exemptions for the very poor and those with small plantings. When the debate ended, the membership chose one of their own to fill the position, Regidor Antonio José Alarí. Three years later, the ayuntamiento changed the procedure, ordering elections for a repartidor in each of the villa's four barrios: San Miguel, Guadalupe, La Muralla, and Torreón. Regidor Gregorio Sanches expressed a hope that, even in times of shortage, the Torreón neighborhood furthest downstream might be allowed a small stream from the Rio Santa Fe for livestock. Someone then responded that, during a drought, animals could seek out what they needed, but fields could not be moved closer to the source of supply.[15]

In addition to allocating water among contending parties, ayuntamientos considered many of the same issues that had vexed governors and alcaldes before independence. Right-of-way problems, for example, recurred frequently. In the spring of 1828, floodwaters from the Rio Chama washed out a large section of the acequia madre at Nuestra Señora de Guadalupe, a small placita several miles above Abiquiú near the mouth of the river's twisting gorge. To determine damages and plan repairs, Alcalde Constitucional José Francisco Vigil and Síndico Procurador Nicolás Archuleta, representatives of the Abiquiú ayuntamiento, met with the acequia's parciantes at the washout. Working together on the ground, they located an appropriate site for a new channel within an adjoining strip of public land. Acting in name of the "Sovereign Mexican Congress," Alcalde Vigil placed the assembled landowners in possession of the ditch course, just as Severino Martín had done for the grantees at La Talaya. After the ceremony, Vigil urged the acequia's parciantes to cooperate in making repairs and to protect their ditch from further damage when disaster threatened.[16]

If a proposed right-of-way crossed private lands instead of public domain, obtaining proper authorization proved much more difficult. A particularly irksome case originated at Santa Cruz in 1829 when Blas Quintana, a resident of the villa, turned to Alcalde Constitucional Matías Ortiz for help in reestablishing his right to use an *acequiacita* or *vena* (lateral ditch). Sixteen years earlier, Quintana had dug the ditch to provide power for a grist mill, after securing right-of-way from Mariano Fresques, since deceased. The arrangement had worked satisfactorily for years until Fresques had taken a sudden dislike to his neighbor and closed off the vena with a plow. Quintana no longer wished to operate the mill, but hoped to irrigate a small plot of crop land and give the produce to religious cofradías to which he belonged. The widow of Fresques, María Estéfana Trujillo, and her truculent children had frustrated this pious wish by refusing to allow the ditch to be reopened. As head of the ayuntamiento, Ortiz had made a personal inspection and had tried to persuade the widow to be reasonable, but he had encountered a hostile reception. Subsequently, the ayuntamiento issued a ruling in Quintana's favor.[17]

Outraged by the decision, Estéfana Trujillo appealed directly to Governor José Antonio Chaves. In a long letter of explanation, she claimed that floods had washed out Quintana's intake during the previous year, but she had denied permission to reopen the little vena because it interfered with the Fresques acequia nearby. Quintana had then sought legal redress from Alcalde Ortiz who, in her eyes, had shirked his duty and failed to uphold the law. Citing provisions in the Mexican constitution that made private property "a sacred thing," she sought assistance from the governor. Chaves sidestepped the situation, however, wisely remanding the cause back to the ayuntamiento to resolve contradictions in the two accounts. During the usual inspection, council members considered the physical characteristics of the river, the two acequias, and adjoining lands at some length. In their decision, the members reiterated that all citizens had rights to irrigation water in times of abundance as long as third parties incurred no damage. Since Quintana had already agreed to make compensation for any injury caused by his ditch, the ayuntamiento reconfirmed his right to use it.[18]

Although the decision involved only a tiny amount of water, it demonstrates that government officials devoted considerable time and attention to the settlement of acequia issues. The case also shows that New Mexico's governors usually regarded the ayuntamientos as the proper agency for the resolution of water problems, and insisted that the councils accept that responsibility. Reconciliation of another dispute several years later at Chimayó, also within the Santa Cruz jurisdiction, reinforces that interpretation. In the summer of 1833, Rafael Espinosa, a citizen from the placita of Nuestra Señora de los Dolores, complained to Governor Francisco Sarracino that José Ortega and Cornelio Vigil of El Potrero had wrongfully relocated the channel of an acequia madre serving the community. Without hesitation, Sarracino sent letters to both parties in which he asserted that the Santa Cruz ayuntamiento, as guardian of the public welfare, must regard acequia regulation as one of its paramount duties.[19] Once informed of Sarracino's ruling, the council quickly convened to hear testimony and determine appropriate action. After a prolonged debate, the members issued a split decision, ordering that the ditch be returned to its old course, despite strident opposition from Diego Pacheco, a disaffected parciante, who threatened to continue irrigating his field through the forbidden channel.[20]

*Alcaldes and Judicial Power*

As presiding officers of the ayuntamientos, alcaldes constitucionales sometimes assumed judicial powers in the course of litigation. Such a situation occurred at Santa Fe in 1831 during a lawsuit between José Victor García and Juan Rafael Ortiz to determine ownership of a farm and water rights in the Pojoaque Valley. A wealthy político, Ortiz had received a one-half interest in the farm in 1815 following the death of his father-in-law, Manuel Delgado, as trustee for his children by Delgado's daughter Estéfana, also deceased. Later, he obtained the other half from his brother-in-law in exchange for a Santa Fe property. On March 16, 1831, Ortiz sold the rancho to García, a valley resident, for 500 pesos. The sales agreement contained a clause, signed by Delgado and his neighbor, Julián Quintana, who had bought part of the adjoining Juan de Mestas grant in 1789, giving García exclusive use of the farm's acequia. When the sale became known, Julián's successor, Antonio Quintana, protested vehemently, claiming that the ditch had washed out previously and been rebuilt under a joint agreement between his family and Delgado. Recently, Ortiz had promised to pay the Quintanas for their work, but had not yet done so. To resolve the matter, don Juan Rafael devised a scheme for retrieving the controversial deed and replacing it with another. While making a social call at García's house and finding the owner absent, he managed to persuade Garcia's wife to surrender the all-important document.[21]

Informed of Ortiz's duplicity, García flew into a rage and filed a complaint with Vicente Martínez, acting alcalde constitucional of Santa Fe's ayuntamiento. Martínez then initiated a process known as *conciliación*, intended to bring about a settlement between the contending parties and avoid a formal trial. Codified in the Spanish constitution of 1812, conciliation was used frequently in New Mexico under Mexican administration, particularly after the governmental reorganization of 1837. Before the proceedings began, each litigant selected an *hombre bueno*—a good man—who served as both advocate and mediator for his client. These persons of high repute were expected to find an area of agreement and arrange a compromise acceptable to both sides.[22] In the case of García v. Ortiz, Alcalde Martínez held an opening hearing on September 29 in which the plaintiff declared that free use of the farm's acequia was the principal issue to be determined. Without that proviso, guaranteed by the deed, the property had little value. After the first session, the hombres buenos set to work, alternately presenting Martínez with written statements in support of their clients. García's representative also collected depositions from witnesses who had seen Ortiz make off with the fateful papers. Eventually, the hombres buenos hammered out a settlement, which was quickly approved by Alcalde Juan García, successor to Martínez. Under its terms, the transaction was canceled; Ortiz took back the farm, returned the purchase price, and received one-third of the crop raised in 1831. Court costs were divided equally.[23] Overshadowing the entire process was a tacit admission by all concerned that farmland without adequate irrigation water was almost unmerchantable.

## Mediation in the Countryside

Once established, the ayuntamientos did not assume all the powers formerly exercised by lesser officials within their jurisdictions. Frequently, alcaldes at small placitas managed to resolve water problems such as acequia maintenance and flood damage without recourse to any higher authority, as illustrated by the following examples.

In 1828, two groups of landowners at Jacona, the heirs of Mateo and Bernardo Roybal, asked the nearest alcalde, Vicente Valdés of San Ildefonso, to determine responsibility for cleaning the upper part of their acequia madre from the intake to the *desagüe,* the system's protective overflow. Mateo and Bernardo, sons of Captain Ignacio Roybal, the Spanish-born soldier whose dealings in land and water at Jacona are discussed in chapter 1—had died many years before. The problem seemed simple enough, but the opposing parties had accumulated a mass of papers through the years as they attempted to reach a final settlement. Valdés recommended that all of them be voided except for a compromise arranged earlier by an alcalde from Santa Cruz that required all landowners to clean the section in question without considering whether their own lands were contiguous.[24] Twenty-six parciantes, half of them Roybals, signed the Valdés agreement, but the problem remained unsolved. Eight years later, in 1836, a successor to Valdés gathered all landowners under "la Acequia Madre de los Señores Roibales de Jacona" and again ordered them to abide by the terms of the Valdés agreement. After more than fifty years, the ditch owners recorded the two documents with the clerk of Santa Fe County—on March 26,

1887, and February 14, 1893, respectively, suggesting that the quarrel persisted for many years.[25]

In May 1834, several residents of Pueblo Quemado (present Córdova) requested similar mediation services from Santa Cruz alcalde Juan Madrid to settle a dispute over a small acequia they had shared for sixteen years. Originating on Romero family lands, and continuing across those of Juan de Jesús Lopes, the ditch had been maintained by Juan Lorenzo Torres, Seledón Córdova, and Juan Pablo Córdova. During the previous July, a cloudburst had flooded the intersecting arroyos and washed out the channel, causing disagreement as to responsibility for cleaning and repairs. The incident had inconvenienced the Romeros and no one wished to offend them further. After looking over the damage, Madrid ordered the landowners jointly to rebuild and maintain the dam at its old location. Henceforth, Lopes would clean from the intake to his property line and the other three would care for the acequia's lower end. To make the settlement binding, Alcalde Madrid imposed the full authority of his office, and the parties agreed that the suit could never be reopened under any circumstances.[26]

Similar difficulties perturbed water users along the Rio Chama. Early in the spring of 1835, overflow from grist mills operated by the Mestas family flooded the acequia madre serving the village of San Antonio (today's El Duende), which seriously delayed necessary maintenance. To correct the situation, Mayordomo Juan Miguel Agüero and his lieutenant complained to the local alcalde, Juan Manuel Vigil, a man who valued his time. Vigil agreed to make an inspection, but when the accusers failed to appear on schedule, he charged them one peso each for wasting the day. During a subsequent visit, he found the charge to be perfectly true, ordered repairs, and collected an embroidered sarape from Asencio Mestas as compensation for his trip.

Several months later, the testy alcalde returned to San Antonio to settle a dispute concerning right-of-way for the acequia's desagüe. A vital part of the irrigation system, the desagüe crossed lands belonging to Juan Pedro de Herrera, who was not a parciante in the ditch. For reasons that are not clear, Herrera had removed a flume from the overflow and replaced it with a channel at ground level. This arrangement did not function as well. When Vigil ordered him to replace the flume "in the name of God and the nation," Herrera replied that he would do so if he could have use of the acequia's sobras, when they were not needed elsewhere, to irrigate a small parcel. Although the bargain seemed fair, the ditch owners objected—until Vigil angrily ordered them to make an agreement within nine days. If they did not, he said, he would himself draw up a document allocating the sobras to Herrera. Evidently, his threat was effective. At the end of his report, the alcalde noted smugly that the grantee had not come to claim the papers.[27]

In addition to mediating maintenance problems, alcaldes also negotiated some of the less acrimonious water allocations, such as those concerning groups of friendly parciantes using the same ditch. An agreement negotiated in 1829 at Desmontes for sixteen newly arrived families led by Juan Ballejos serves as a case in point. Anxious to obtain farmlands, the prospective settlers had petitioned for a tract outside the area developed by Felipe Gonzales and Mariano Sanches, but they needed a dependable water supply before committing themselves to stay. To that end, they asked the veteran alcalde Juan Antonio Lovato to help them reach a satisfactory accord with Gonzales and other owners of the Cuchilla ditch. After some bargaining, the latter agreed to permit Ballejos and his compañeros to share the acequia under certain conditions: (1) they must make an irrevocable commitment to widen the ditch and perform a proportionate share of regular maintenance; (2) they must recognize that the original owners had a prior right to six surcos of water at all times; and (3) the Ballejos group must divert their share through a separate lateral. With those stipulations accepted by both sides, the alcalde drew up a formal document. Duly signed, witnessed, and ratified, the agreement has endured remarkably. On November 17, 1887, it was recorded by the clerk of Taos County; on December 9, 1959, officers of the Desmontes acequias used the pact to substantiate their declaration of ownership of water rights with the State Engineer office.[28]

When quarrels over water disrupted the community, alcaldes sometimes resorted to extreme measures to restore harmony. A situation of that kind unfolded at Cuyamungué in 1831 among members of the Valdés family following the death of their mother, Andrea Lucero, who had accumulated a substantial estate. A son, Vicente Valdés gradually enlarged his inheritance by buying small parcels of farmland from the other heirs. As the neighborhood's leading property owner, Valdés also became mayordomo of an important ditch, La Acequia de los Ojitos, which originated on Tesuque Pueblo lands. Before long, his brothers and sisters complained to authorities in Santa Cruz that Vicente abused his office by usurping more than his share of water ; he was, they said, generally riding roughshod over them. After several months of dissension, Alcalde Juan Gallego fired the troublemaking mayordomo, an extraordinary step, and then approved election of his brother, Juan Valdés, as a replacement. To restore peace among the parciantes, Gallego ordered the new incumbent to divide the acequia's flow according to need and severely punish anyone who increased his allotment by blocking the ditch. As for the deposed don Vicente, his legitimate rights were to be fully protected in times of both shortage and plenty, without prejudice.[29]

If rulings like Gallego's seemed arbitrary or unfair, those aggrieved retained the right of appeal to the governor. Soon after he assumed office in 1827, Governor Manuel Armijo received petitions from two victims of decisions handed down impulsively by alcaldes in water disputes. The first, originating in the Rio Abajo region, came from José Miguel Aragón, who represented the people of Corrales in litigation with two family groups upstream, the Montoyas and the Tenorios, over water from the Rio Grande. As feelings intensified, a local official had arrested Aragón for questioning an order that established procedures for hearing the case. Hoping to be liberated, the Corrales man blamed his difficulties on legal maneuvers by Antonio Ruiz, apoderado (legal representative) of the opposing parties. Artfully, Aragón asserted that the governor should not be bothered with such trivia and that the case could be settled in a local court. After explaining away the controversial remarks that had caused him so much trouble, and denying some false statements made by Ruiz, Aragón proposed a compromise acceptable to his clients. Under its terms, the two parties would exchange portions of the acequia system serving their lands, alterations that would ensure an equitable distribution. In closing, he declared his devotion to the cause of justice and implored Armijo to heed his plea. A marginal notation on Aragon's petition indicates that the governor took some action a few days later, but the details of his response are no longer extant.[30]

Within a month, Armijo faced a similar problem with a local official at the rough-and-tumble frontier village of San Miguel del Vado on the Rio Pecos. Controversy began when the wife of a prominent citizen, Manuel Antonio Baca, brought charges against Santiago Ulibarrí for illegal diversion of water from the Pecos, thus short-circuiting the acequia madre that served Baca's rancho. During a hearing before Alcalde Gregorio Vigil, Gabriel Domínguez, an employee of Baca's, testified that he had seen the accused and three of his servants reopen a channel into his land. The channel had been previously closed off by debris from a flood. Ulibarrí denied the allegation and expressed rage that Domínguez, whom he described as a "knavish rogue" (pícaro arrastrado), should be accorded greater credibility than he, a man of substance, "well-known in this and other provinces." As the discussion became more heated, Ulibarrí insulted the alcalde, who then threw him in jail. From his place of confinement, the prisoner sought relief by writing a long petition to Governor Armijo, expressing his shame and indignation. Reacting sympathetically, the governor ordered Ulibarrí's immediate release and directed Vigil to prepare a detailed report of the circumstances leading up to his incarceration. In a dignified reply, the alcalde ably defended himself, arguing that Ulibarrí's attack on his character had been unacceptable and had set a bad example for the community. A record of the final disposition of the case is not extant, but within two years Ulibarrí himself held office as San Miguel's alcalde, a fact that suggests his reputation was not affected.[31]

## Role of the Governor

As shown by the two preceding incidents, in the Mexican era New Mexicans who believed they had been wronged by local officials could continue to turn to the governor for assistance, just as during the colonial period. Under the new government, however, the governor's authority to dismiss popularly elected alcaldes constitucionales for incompetence or insubordination was less clear. Another occurrence at San Miguel del Vado will illustrate the point.

In March 1824, Governor Bartolomé Baca, finding himself at odds with San Miguel's alcalde, Diego Padilla, decided to handpick a replacement—an event that caused deep resentment among the free-spirited settlers. Soon thereafter, drummers in the plaza beat out a rousing tattoo to call the citizenry together for a public meeting at the village *casa consistorial* (town hall). After some fiery oratory, in which members of the ayuntamiento denied the governor's power to remove an official chosen by the people, the crowd returned Padilla to office and presented him with the *bastón* (cane) symbolizing his authority. When news of this outburst reached Santa Fe, Baca immediately sent Santiago Abreu, a trusted troubleshooter, to San Miguel with orders to investigate and suggest appropriate action. At the scene of the insurrection, Abreu interrogated the ringleaders, who had all been identified by Baca's henchman, and determined that the incident represented a serious affront to the government. As an example to future troublemakers, he recommended that Padilla and the dissident council members be fired and fined a hefty fifty pesos each. Smaller levies were assessed against the drummers and a few minor participants, bringing the matter to a close.[32] Despite the severity of his punishment, Padilla, like Ulibarrí, suffered only briefly from the confrontation with higher-ups: by October, he was again San Miguel's alcalde.

When neither alcaldes or ayuntamientos could forge an agreement, aggrieved parties might request intervention by the governor. A situation of that kind troubled relations between Las Trampas and Las Truchas during a quarrel over water from the Rito San Leonardo, a tiny creek rising high in the Sangre de Cristos. Soon after first settlement, Trampaseños made plans to divert the stream for irrigation in the Cañada del Ojo Sarco, a proposal vigorously opposed by residents of Truchas, who claimed an exclusive right. Ruling that Ojo Sarco was suitable for grazing only, in 1755 Governor Vélez Cachupín issued a decree favoring Truchas, but the question was not to be resolved so easily.[33]

After a long period of relative calm, in 1836 the feud began again with renewed intensity. Objecting to efforts by Trampas citizens to farm at Ojo Sarco, Juan Antonio Fernández and José Apolinario Vigil filed a formal protest on behalf of Las Truchas with Governor Albino Pérez. Submitting appropriate documentation, the petitioners stated that Ojo Sarco's fields could be irrigated only with water that Truchas had preempted many years earlier—a supply they had maintained with great effort. They asked Pérez to inform the Trampas ayuntamiento of Truchas's prior right and for him to discourage further development at Ojo Sarco. Not to be outdone, the Trampas people produced a 1768 document that revoked Truchas's exclusive rights in the San Leonardo and allowed them to use its water for irrigation. Confronted with such strong evidence, Pérez declared that the stream's flow was "free" (*libre*) and available for use by Ojo Sarco farmers.[34]

The governor's decision caused hard feelings, of course. Four years later, Mariano Lucero, juez de paz at San Juan, received a disturbing statement from Juan Pablo Córdova, of Truchas—the Córdova involved in another water dispute at Pueblo Quemado in 1834, discussed before in this chapter. In his deposition, Córdova said that he and several compañeros had encountered Juan Antonio Baca and Tomás Domínguez from Las Trampas while resting at a *jacal* on their grant. When asked where they were going, the two replied that they intended to turn water into the Ojo Sarco acequia and that, if their documents failed to establish their rights, they would resort to force of arms. Later, Córdova and two others from Truchas attempted to return the water to their own ditch, but were stopped by gruff Trampaseños, who said they would give it up only at gunpoint. After the face-off, both sides appealed to Lucero for a ruling, each again presenting their papers. Having reviewed the case, Lucero reaffirmed Governor Pérez's judgment and ruled further that Trampas had exclusive right to water from the San Leonardo.[35] As in the dispute at Taos concerning the Rio Lucero, violence was narrowly avoided, but, as at Taos, the case was not settled and was reopened during the territorial period.

### After the Siete Leyes

Although officials sometimes seemed indecisive and squabbled among themselves, during the first years of Mexican rule the agencies of local government usually managed to resolve problems within their jurisdictions. With few exceptions, the system responded to public opinion and recognized the importance of accepted customs in water administration. Changes came in 1836, however, when the conservative political faction came to power in Mexico and imposed a centralist constitution known as the Siete Leyes. New legislation divided the nation into departments and reorganized the three branches of government. Elevated to departmental status, New Mexico was partitioned into two districts, the Rio Arriba and the Rio Abajo, each administered by a prefect responsible to the governor. Regarded as dangerously democratic, the ayuntamientos were again abolished, except for the one in Santa Fe. Many former council responsibilities passed to the prefects and to a new class of local officeholders known as juezes de paz.[36] Although never popular in New Mexico, the departmental plan remained in place until the United States conquest in 1846, and the local offices created by the centralists continued into the territorial era. The new government made significant changes in judicial procedures, increasing usage of the conciliation process considered above. In an attempt to curtail unnecessary litigation, an act passed on May 23, 1837 required aggrieved parties to carry out a non-binding conciliation before a juez prior to beginning a lawsuit.[37]

Sometimes groups of parciantes who used the same acequia employed conciliation to work out a simple maintenance agreement—pacts similar to those considered above. In 1844, on orders from a superior, Juez de Paz Gervasio Ortega of Santa Cruz assembled the residents of La Mesilla and Polvadera, two placitas below the villa, to establish an annual labor schedule for their jointly owned ditch. Although the two communities had tried unsuccessfully to resolve the issue for a long time, Ortega and the hombres buenos managed to negotiate a settlement that determined mutual responsibilities and imposed acceptable penalties for infractions. Declaring that the pact was to last for the rest of their lives, the litigants made sure that Ortega recorded it in the villa's archives. Several decades later, on April 3, 1897, a slightly different version of the same document was presented to the clerk of Santa Fe County for registration—an indication that the settlement remained in force well beyond the lifetimes of the original signatories.[38]

By participating in conciliation, hombres buenos helped resolve water disputes in ways that conformed to community values, but, since it was not binding, the process did not always go smoothly. At the placita of San Antonio de Chama in 1838, for example, agents of two adversarial parties agreed on an appropriate location for a grist mill on la Acequia Común de los Salazares, an important ditch emanating from the Rio Chama. At the last minute, however, as the presiding justice collected signatures from the litigants and witnesses, the deal collapsed: one of the principals had changed his mind. To express dissatisfaction further, this litigant dismissed his hombre bueno, who happened to be his son-in-law—a circumstance that must have provoked some lively family conversation.[39]

Frequently when negotiations broke down in justice courts, the litigants turned to the prefect, or even the governor, for help in finding an accommodation. A case heard at Abiquiú in 1841 before Juez de Paz José María Chaves illustrates some of the pitfalls inherent in conciliation. One of Abiquiú's most famous sons, Chaves was a rising politico, then in the midst of a long career in which he held civil and military offices under Spain, Mexico, and the United States. Controversy began after José Francisco Vigil, a local farmer, built a protective dike on his property to prevent inundation of some fields with waste water whenever neighbors above began to irrigate. Ordinarily, the structure did not cause problems, but when cloudbursts filled nearby arroyos and breached the acequia, Vigil's dike trapped much of the runoff and forced it back onto the plantings of Miguel Antonio Gallegos and Diego de Luna. Seeking relief, the latter appealed to Chaves, who set a hearing date and ordered the concerned parties to appear with their hombres buenos as required by law. When the two sides gathered, the juez found that the hombres buenos, like their clients, could not agree on the dike's future status, causing Chaves to recess the proceedings for eight days while he made a decision. Once reconvened, the court ruled that, as a free man, Vigil had a right to protect his property, and thus, could maintain a dike of moderate size to prevent flooding. Chaves added arbitrarily that the plaintiffs would not be allowed further appeal. All parties signed the decree, but Gallegos and Luna added the phrase *"no soy conforme"* (I do not agree) next to their names.[40]

Still smarting from the Chaves verdict, Gallegos and Luna sought redress directly from Rio Arriba's prefect, Juan Andrés Archuleta. Demonstrating some knowledge of the law, they bolstered their plea with references to technical deficiencies in the adverse ruling, which they attributed to bias by the juez. Many times, they claimed, local justices acted capriciously, knowing that final appeal rested with the supreme court in far-off Mexico City. As a remedy, they begged the prefect to assert jurisdiction and remand their case to an impartial juez.[41]

Archuleta's ruling is not extant; however, he is known to have at times allowed litigation to bog down in bureaucratic red tape. One such case dragged on for more than three years. It began simply enough in April 1841 at San Pedro de Chamita when Juan de Jesús Córdova asked several neighbors for a right-of-way across their lands for an acequia to provide water power at a new grist mill. In return, he offered to grind their grain free of charge. All the neighbors proved to be willing except José Rafael Trujillo, who feared extensive damage to his property. To end the impasse, Santa Clara's juez de paz and census taker, Juan Cristóbal García, arranged a conciliation attended by Córdova, Trujillo, and their good men. At the end of a long discussion, Trujillo authorized the ditch, but he made some very specific stipulations: Córdova had to promise to reinforce the acequia's intake and to curb overflows along the lower bank by building it up with rocks and branches to Trujillo's satisfaction; if floods caused significant destruction in spite of these precautions, Córdova had to make restitution for losses incurred along the first fifty varas of right-of-way, the amount to be determined by the nearest justice. Córdova agreed, and after all parties had signed the document, García placed Córdova in possession of the ditch.[42]

Trujillo soon found that he had made a bad bargain. On February 16, 1843, he complained to Prefect Archuleta that the new acequia leaked from one end to the other, causing damage well beyond the first fifty varas, and to his dismay, Córdova refused to provide compensation. As usual, Archuleta referred the matter back to the juez (now Rafael García, Juan Cristóbal's successor at Santa Clara), who, together with four advisers, inspected the ditch and found Trujillo's claim entirely justified.[43] Córdova's position worsened even more after he refused to pay the experts a fee of twelve pesos for their trip, causing García to lock him in the stocks.[44]

Still not convinced, and perhaps unwilling to overturn the original agreement, Archuleta ordered another opinion from the juez at San Juan. Meanwhile,

Córdova's relatives fired off a series of impassioned petitions to the prefect, intimating bias and protesting the harsh treatment suffered by their kinsman. Archuleta then ordered Manuel Morfín, the juez at San Juan, to take charge of the case, but, on April 28, Juez García called the parties before him and commanded Córdova to close off his acequia.[45] Belatedly, Morfín held a hearing but refused to overturn the decision of another juez, and for the next year, the Córdovas, trying in vain to settle this simple case in a local court, were unable to find a justice willing to assume responsibility. Then in July 1844, Juan de Jesús Córdova presented the whole matter before Mariano Martínez de Lejanza, who had taken office as New Mexico's civil governor in January. Appalled by Córdova's tale of repeated delays and shoddy procedures by local justices, Martínez handed the case over to Tomás Ortiz, a Santa Fe alcalde, with directions to arrange a hearing immediately and find an equitable solution. The governor also sharply reprimanded every justice involved, observing that they had failed utterly in carrying out their responsibilities and demanding improved performance in the future. Within a few days, Ortiz notified his superior that the parties had met, reached a new agreement, and ended the lawsuit.[46]

In his statement, the governor reserved his criticism for the local justices, but Archuleta, too, should have shared some of the blame. If he had acted more decisively, he could have saved considerable delay and prevented his subordinates from evading their responsibilities. However, in another case from the same jurisdiction, the prefect performed with greater assurance. On September 3, 1838, Jesús María Manzanares, of San Juan de Chama (today's Plaza Larga), composed a long letter to Archuleta in which he requested atonement for public abuse by the community mayordomo, Pedro Herrera. According to Manzanares, he—Manzanares—had gone to Herrera's house in place of his younger brother, who had been ordered to present himself there. When Jesús María asked why the summons had been issued, the mayordomo replied that he had intended to punish the younger Manzanares, but, in his absence, the older brother would do just as well. Harsh words escalated into a scuffle, and Herrera had Jesús María tied up, subjecting him to public humiliation. Further investigation revealed that young Manzanares had refused to pay a fee of one peso to the mayordomo prior to receiving irrigation water, a practice described by Jesús María as an illegal sale.

In reply, Archuleta sagely observed that, although no one could properly assault a duly appointed official, those in authority must not resort to bribery while performing their duties. He ordered the juez at Santa Clara to verify the facts, and then, if warranted, to fine Herrera ten pesos in hard cash—five for the district treasury, and five for Manzanares. When notified of the penalty imposed against him, Herrera was stunned by its severity. As a poor man, he appealed to the prefect's sense of charity, claiming that his misdeeds resulted from lack of understanding rather than ill will. If the heavy fine must be paid, he begged that it be in "products of the country" (*efectos del país*), rather than in money. As an afterthought, he added that the so-called water sale was a procedure authorized by the acequia's *principales,* who supervised its management. If the peso demanded by the mayordomo was an assessment rather than a user's fee or bribe, it was an unusual charge for that time—one not recognized as such by either Archuleta or Manzanares. In this instance, the prefect ended the suit summarily by directing the juez to proceed as ordered, waiving the requirement for a cash payment.[47]

As indicated by the previous discussion, institutions of local government changed significantly under Mexican administration, but water regulation problems remained much the same as those encountered during the colonial era. A growing population accelerated competition for arable land and irrigation water between Hispanos and Pueblo Indians and between contending groups of Hispano settlers. Allocations and related issues were determined by community ayuntamientos until these councils were abolished in 1837, and juezes de paz assumed similar responsibilities. Aggrieved parties often complained of bias by officials in their jurisdictions, an inevitable problem in an area of small villages with highly interrelated populations. Dissatisfied litigants often sought redress from the governor or prefect, but those officials preferred to remand water cases back to local authorities whenever possible. An appeal to the nation's highest tribunal, the supreme court in Mexico City, although sometimes considered, was never attempted, according to available documentary sources. Despite frequent complaints, New Mexicans managed to resolve most water problems locally, relying more on local customs than law books in arranging settlements.

Fig. 1. Bisecting the state as it flows south, the mighty Rio Grande has provided farmers with irrigation water for centuries. This aerial view shows cultivated fields near the river's junction with the Rio Santa Fe, visible at upper right. The area has been under water since construction of the Cóchiti Dam began in 1965. Courtesy Rio Grande Historical Collections, Yeo Collection, New Mexico State University Library.

Fig. 4. A farm family east of the Sangre de Cristo Mountains, 1895. Courtesy Museum of New Mexico, neg. no. 22468.

(Above left) Fig. 2. From the colonial era to the present, the community acequia has been the preeminent institution for water management in New Mexico. The ditch pictured here irrigates fields in the Rio Abajo region below Albuquerque. Courtesy Museum of New Mexico, William H. Cobb, neg. no. 15141.

Fig. 3. Northern New Mexico rancho, Chama Valley near Abiquiú. The fields and orchard in the background receive water from the Rio Chama. Courtesy Museum of New Mexico, neg. no. 5182.

Fig. 5. Although local farmers usually raised adequate crops, Anglo visitors to New Mexico regarded their implements and agricultural techniques as hopelessly old-fashioned. Here, a matched pair of roan oxen pull a wooden plow at El Prado (Los Estiércoles) near Taos. From the collection of the Kit Carson Historic Museums.

(*Above right*) Fig. 6. Once fields were seeded in the spring, a thorough irrigation helped to establish emerging plants. Children learned traditional skills by tagging along. Courtesy Museum of New Mexico, neg. no. 58868.

7. Watered from an adjoining ditch, the crop of this *milpa* (corn field) near Santa Fe is almost ready to harvest. Courtesy Museum of New Mexico, neg. no. 5542.

8. After stacking new-cut grain, farmers drove herds of horses, sheep, or goats around the heaped up pile to separate kernels of wheat, barley, or oats from the straw. Flour made from wheat processed in that way was often gritty. Courtesy Museum of New Mexico, neg. no. 12583.

9. Additional chaff was sometimes removed with a *criba* (sieve or sifter). Courtesy Museum of New Mexico, neg. no. 5072.

10. Diversion dams for irrigation ditches were made of rocks, brush and sod. Spring flooding often demolished them. Courtesy Museum of New Mexico, neg. no. 5544.

11. Before the construction of flood control dams along the Rio Grande, high water frequently inundated large areas such as these fields between Bernalillo and Albuquerque. Courtesy Rio Grande Historical Collections, Yeo Collection, New Mexico State University Library.

12. To carry water across intervening arroyos, irrigators sometimes used logs to build flumes similar to this one on the Acequia de los Espinosas near Chimayó. Courtesy Museum of New Mexico, neg. no. 9051.

13. This Rio Arriba farmer is taking water from the main acequia to irrigate his planting through a crude *toma* (headgate) made from a hollowed log. Courtesy Museum of New Mexico, Hazen, neg. no. 5541.

14. In south-central New Mexico, competition for water was particularly intense at Tularosa, a small village west of the Sacramento Mountains. In 1887, farmers plowed a field up to the doorway of the town's hotel. Courtesy Rio Grande Historical Collections, Blazer Family Papers, New Mexico State University Library.

15. Near the end of the nineteenth century, entrepreneurs promoted massive water projects in New Mexico requiring huge expenditures and sophisticated technology. Complex structures, such as the Elephant Butte Dam, pictured here, contrasted sharply with the small-scale irrigation works used by Hispano farmers. Courtesy Rio Grande Historical Collections, New Mexico State University Library.

18. Extending toward the horizon, this young peach orchard at Carlsbad exemplifies the agricultural expansion that became possible through innovations in irrigation. Courtesy Museum of New Mexico, neg. no. 57848.

(*Above left*) 16. The new irrigation projects depended on enormous canals. Drawing water from the Rio Pecos, this one is located near Carlsbad. Courtesy Museum of New Mexico, neg. no. 58889.

17. Modern machinery facilitated excavation and maintenance of channels and diversions. Here, a steam-powered dragline enlarges the east side canal in Doña Ana County. Courtesy Rio Grande Historical Collections, New Mexico State University Library.

# 4 | Water Administration During the Early Territorial Era

AₗₜₕₒᵤGH NEVER POPULAR in New Mexico, the departmental plan imposed by the centralist party in 1836–1837 remained in place until United States forces invaded the region in 1846. Following the annexation of Texas, tension between the United States and Mexico culminated in a border skirmish near Matamoros on April 25. Congress issued a declaration of war on May 11 and, in late June, Brigadier General Stephen Watts Kearny led 1,600 troops out of Fort Leavenworth in order to subjugate New Mexico and California. After crossing the plains, Kearny's men marched into the Santa Fe plaza late in the afternoon of August 18, bringing an end to Mexican sovereignty and running up the Stars and Stripes over the Palace of the Governors. The conquest had been accomplished without firing a shot. Before leaving for California, Kearny designated New Mexico as a United States territory and appointed a governor, judges, and other officials as an interim administration. He also promulgated a hastily assembled collection of U.S. and Mexican laws, popularly known as the Kearny Code (considered in more detail later in this chapter). The following January, some localized conflict occurred near Taos and Mora, but most New Mexicans accepted the change in government without resistance.[1]

In the wake of the conquest, a number of Anglo-American opportunists and sightseers made their way into New Mexico, some of whom recorded their impressions of life in what was to them a remote and exotic region. Early arrivals included Lewis H. Garrard, a greenhorn of seventeen who had traveled from Cincinnati for a look at the so-called Wild West. Garrard was a careful observer and he later recalled his experiences in a book entitled *Wah-To-Yah and the Taos Trail*. He first reached Taos on a chilly day in early April 1847, with a small party of Anglo mountain men and United States soldiers who crossed over the Sangre de Cristo range through Palo Flechado Pass and descended into the Rio Fernando Canyon. They arrived about three months after the suppression of the Taos rebellion, high point of the belated nationalistic protest against the U.S. invasion.

In his book, Garrard focused on the subsequent trials and executions of Pueblo Indian and Mexican rebels, but he also digressed to describe the local culture, including the Taos Valley's acequia system. His report was one of the first by an outsider to recognize the importance to New Mexico of irrigation, noting, in his account of the party's emergence from the canyon into agricultural lands bordering the Rio Fernando:

> The brook down which channel we had kept the preceding few hours, was, at its egress, directed into a large "acequia," or ditch, and from that in numberless small ones, through the valley to serve in lieu of the grateful showers in which the American farmer puts so much dependence.[2]

Garrard's ditch must have been either the Acequia del Norte or the Acequia del Sur del Cañón, both of which emanate from the Rio Fernando and both of which are still in use. After passing a distillery that converted local wheat into the ever popular *aguardiente de Taos,* the travelers saw workmen giving an acequia its annual cleaning under the watchful eye of their mayordomo.

During his brief visit, Garrard learned that the valley's fertile soil yielded a generous return from the seed planted. Although handicapped by primitive implements, Taos farmers produced good crops of wheat and corn. Concerning irrigation, Garrard wrote:

> The valley, in every direction, was cultivated, and in the total absence of fences, presented the unusual sight of one large field, stretching away for miles, intersected by numberless ditches. The melting snow from the mountains flows to the valley, where it is turned into large acequias; from there into branches, and again through each man's possession. When a plat needs watering, the ditch below it is stopped with a few shovelsful of earth, water suffered to flow in, and, there being no egress, it inundates the plat, thereby giving the vegetation a more effectual and well-timed flooding than the uncertain showers. This seems a preferable mode; for the ditch, once dug, with an occasional cleaning, serves forever. When it does need scraping out, the alcalde, or mayor, issues an order, and the work is done by the people conjointly; so the labor is but slight to any one man.[3]

Published in 1850 to favorable reviews, Garrard's book was one of many memoirs written soon after the Mexican War by various participants. At the end of hostilities, officials in Washington eagerly awaited detailed information concerning the resources of the regions recently annexed. Although the federal bureaucracy did not yet include a department of agriculture, Congress had given responsibility for gathering farm data to an unlikely agency: the United States Patent Office. Each year, the commissioner of patents distributed questionnaires to state and territorial governors, who in turn passed them along to knowledgeable persons within their jurisdictions. The commissioner asked for information about annual yields and production costs for wheat, corn, cotton, hay, and other commodities, fertilizer use, insect infestations, plant diseases, crop rotation, sales prices, and care and management of livestock. Data from the returns were printed in the agency's annual report.[4] Many questions did not apply to New Mexico, of course, but the responses submitted in 1851 and 1852 provide valuable information as to the state of agriculture in the new territory at that time. They also offer an interesting contrast to the report compiled a decade earlier under Mexican administration by Juan Cristóbal García at Santa Clara.

In 1851, James S. Calhoun, New Mexico's recently appointed governor, sent out copies of the commissioner's questionnaire to his "experts": Manuel Alvarez, a Spanish-born merchant and former U.S. consul at Santa Fe; Spruce M. Baird, a Texas attorney and politico who had recently established a hacienda below Albuquerque; and John Fox Hammond, a young army doctor with service at Socorro and Doña Ana. A year later, Calhoun's successor, William Carr Lane, contented himself with enlisting a single reporter for the entire territory: Dr. Thomas E. Massie, a discharged veteran of the recent wars who had opened a private medical practice in Santa Fe.[5] Together, the four accounts present a comprehensive description of irrigated agriculture along the valley of the Rio Grande and its tributaries.[6]

All four reporters emphasized the importance of irrigation, a technique unfamiliar to most United States farmers at that time. Massie went so far as to say:

> Speaking in an agricultural sense, land in this country is nothing, and water is *everything.* Lands in the states without running water have value; lands in New Mexico without water are without value to the agriculturist. There is not a single crop of the husbandman that can be produced in this country with any degree of certainty without irrigation.

Baird agreed, adding that, while farmers along the Rio Grande were fortunate to have a reliable water supply readily available, a few well-timed showers during the growing season improved yields significantly. All four noted that irrigation, for the most part, served as a substitute for fertilizers, such as manure, which was rarely used in New Mexico, or bat guano, a product completely unknown there. According to Hammond, the cost of labor needed for irrigation constituted the largest expense in raising a crop.

Each correspondent devoted considerable attention to specific procedures for growing wheat and corn in his area. Most farmers began the crop year by flooding their fields to prepare the soil for plowing and provide moisture to sprout the seed. Once watered, the lands were ready for the plow, a crude device made entirely of wood except for an iron point on the share. Even with that reinforcement, New Mexican plows rarely penetrated the earth more than two or three inches. A few improved models made of steel had been imported from the East with good results, but high costs had prevented their general use. Both wheat and corn were sown much more sparingly than in other regions, but the yield did not seem to be adversely effected. After being broadcast by hand, wheat seed was plowed under. The surface was then harrowed and smoothed with a light log, drawn by oxen. Farmers planted corn in furrows about six feet apart, dropping five or six kernels into the ground at intervals of three to six feet. Beans were often grown in the wider spaces. During the summer, the plants were cultivated, hoed for weeds, and irrigated when necessary, depending on rainfall and the water supply.

Although very old, fields seldom lay fallow; those close to the early settlements had been in production for 150 or 200 years with only occasional respite. Crop rotation consisted only of alternating corn and wheat. It was a seemingly unending cycle; nevertheless, thanks to irrigation, the land continued to produce respectable crops. Both Hammond and Baird observed that landholders in the Rio Abajo rarely fenced their farmlands, employing herders to prevent wandering livestock from intruding.

At the end of the growing season, everyone began the harvest simultaneously, on orders from the alcalde, who ignored differences in the maturity of particular plots. Once the crops had been gathered by the whole community working day and night, the same official set a time for allowing animals into the cutover fields, which were then grazed in common. Like the implements used for tilling the soil, harvest technology was primitive. New Mexico ranchers cut wheat (and probably corn stalks, too) with a sickle, a time-consuming task. Technological breakthroughs such as the scythe and cradle were as yet unknown in the territory. To begin separating wheat from chaff, livestock, usually horses or goats, tramped around a great pile of sheaves heaped up on an earthen floor. Later, the farm family continued the process by tossing the partially cleaned grain high in the air on windy days, allowing the breeze to carry off most of the straw. Finally, pebbles and other trash were extracted by shaking the wheat through a large sieve, made of rawhide with small holes burned through that retained most of the impurities, allowing the grain to fall out, ready for storage.

In addition to describing field crops, Hammond also included an interesting survey of viniculture and wine manufacture in the Rio Abajo region, where these industries had a long history. Propagated by transplanting roots or setting out cuttings, grape vines were planted about six feet apart and grew to a height of three or four feet, yielding their first fruit during the second or third season. At Socorro, Hammond reported, growers carefully heaped earth around each vine in the fall to protect them from killing frosts; at Doña Ana, such precautions were unnecessary. Early in March, the dirt was shoveled away and shaped into channels to prepare the fields for irrigation. Pruning, to remove dead branches and cut back excess growth from the previous year, followed. When the grapes ripened, in September, growers picked the best bunches for wine, placing them in the shade for several days before beginning the celebrated process of pressing the soggy mass through a leather sieve with bare feet. Subsequently, vintners strained the skins from the must, which was then boiled and placed in rawhide vats for fermentation. When ready, the wine was drawn off for storage in casks or porous earthen jars until approved for consumption. The lesser quality grapes were used for *aguardiente,* or brandy, made in similar fashion except that the product was distilled at the end of the process.

Although the patent office discontinued publication of the agricultural portion of its yearly report after 1852, the documents cited above are sufficient to suggest that New Mexico's farmers maintained an adequate level of crop production without benefit of the technological innovations gaining acceptance in other parts of the nation. According to reports from local observers, their success resulted in large measure from irrigation, a sine qua non for agriculture in the Southwest. Continuation of procedures for equitable water administration thus was a prime concern of the newly formed territorial government.

### Adaptation to U.S. Laws

As initiated in 1846, the Kearny Code provided New Mexico with an executive, a court system, and an elected legislative assembly. At the local level, the code established county governments to be directed by prefects and alcaldes, offices retained from the Mexican era, who were appointed by the governor. Prefects served as county administrators and also had the duties of probate judges under Anglo-U.S. law. For water management, a catch-all section at the end of the code provided that "laws concerning water courses, stock marks and brands, horses, enclosures, commons, and arbitrations shall continue in force," with the stipulation that powers of the ayuntamientos passed to the prefects and alcaldes.[7] The code's authors forgot that ayuntamientos had been defunct for ten years, except for the one in Santa Fe.

In the fall of 1846, when news of Kearny's actions reached Washington, irate congressional leaders complained to President James K. Polk that, in making New Mexico a territory, the general had infringed on their prerogatives. As a gesture of conciliation, on December 22 Polk delivered a message to the House of Representatives in which he repudiated those sections of the Kearny Code granting territorial status. Although the code's other provisions remained in force, several years of confusion ensued, during which New Mexico suffered under a military government that demonstrated little concern for civil rights. Congress rectified the situation on September 9, 1850, by passing the Organic Act—part of the great, intersectional Compromise of 1850. Under the act's terms, New Mexico regained its position as a United States territory and civilian government was restored.[8] The new legislation also provided that the offices of prefect and alcalde be renamed as probate judge and justice of the peace, but their duties remained unchanged.[9] In 1851, the first session of the territorial legislature made the two positions elective.[10]

Once a government had been organized, native New Mexicans faced the problem of adapting the newly imposed institutions to their traditional culture. How could they shape this unfamiliar and rather exotic system in advantageous ways? Throughout much of the territory, New Mexicans managed to achieve that objective quite successfully for several decades. Since popular elections determined distribution of legislative seats and local offices, members of the Hispano elite, not surprisingly, almost always emerged victorious. Once elected, justices of the peace and probate judges functioned in much the same way as juezes de paz and prefectos had done under Mexican rule, which smoothed the transition. Although spheres of jurisdiction between the two offices were not always clear, justice of the peace courts usually provided the original venue for litigating water issues. Local juezes left few records of their activities during the early territorial period, but those that remain give some insight into the issues considered.

Under terms of an act passed by the territorial legislature on January 7, 1852, justices of the peace became responsible for conducting elections to choose mayordomos for each ditch in their communities.[11] An event of that kind took place in the spring of 1867 at Rincón de Tecolote, a small village in San Miguel County near present Rociada, where the citizenry gathered on April 7 to name overseers for three principal acequias. Once tabulated, the results were duly recorded in the juez's docket. The same legislation made the justices responsible for hearing complaints brought by mayordomos against recalcitrant users for such infractions as refusing work assignments, preempting water without permission, or questioning the overseer's authority. When the need arose, justice was swift. On July 16, 1859, for example, Mayordomo Eulogio Gonzales initiated an action in the local court at Rincón de Tecolote against Pablo Jaramillo who was accused of resisting a legal order. Without delay, Juez de Paz Nazario Gonzales ordered the accused apprehended for arraignment, heard testimony from witnesses, and fined Jaramillo one peso—all on the same day. Proper procedure was important in determining settlements, however. In a case involving illegal water appropriation in San Miguel County, the presiding justice dismissed the suit because the plaintiff had complained only to the mayordomo and had not asked the defendant to desist, a necessary prerequisite for legal action.[12]

In addition to adjudicating petty suits, justices of the peace also used their authority to validate water agreements arranged out of court. At Jarales, a placita below Belén in the Rio Abajo, for example, Juez de Paz Bernardino Torres recorded a contract drawn up in 1859 between parciantes of the community's acequia madre and José María Sanches that allowed the latter to locate a grist mill on their ditch. In return, Sanches committed himself to grind grain for the acequia's owners at a reduced fee: two reales per fanega for wheat, three for corn. He also agreed to run the mill only when the mayordomo determined that surplus water was available. For their part, the parciantes promised to help with maintenance in the mill ditch to qualify for his lowered rates and allowed Sanches to grind for others whenever they did not require his services. To make the agreement official, Torres drew up the necessary document and arranged to have it recorded in the county records.[13]

More important water litigation went before county probate judges through original jurisdiction or on appeal from justices' courts. Probate rulings, in turn, could be appealed to district court, the next rung on the judicial ladder. Under powers mandated by the Kearny Code and the Organic Act, probate judges not only supervised administration of wills and estates but also served as the county executive, determining election procedures, directing road maintenance, and disbursing county funds. Soon after the establishment of territorial government, the post of *el prefecto* (probate judge) became a political plum usually reserved for members of the *rico* class.[14] At the first election held in Taos County, voters chose José María Martínez, son of a former alcalde, Severino Martínez, and younger brother of the famed Mexican nationalist priest, Antonio José Martínez. Subsequently, the position often served as a stepping-stone for those who aspired to higher office. Antonio Joseph, who later represented New Mexico in Congress for ten years, served as Taos County's probate judge for three terms from 1875 to 1881. Significantly, only one Anglo was elected to that office at Taos prior to 1890. The lone exception was Horace ("Oracio") Long, a shadowy figure who had arrived in the 1830s, probably as a fur trapper. After converting to Roman Catholicism, Long married a local girl and began raising a large family, indications that he had been well-acculturated before assuming the bench in 1855.[15]

In Taos County, water apportionment between competing communities proved to be the most difficult problem confronting probate judges. During court sessions, prefects attempted to resolve several long-standing water disputes, some of which had originated years earlier during the Mexican era. To reach decisions, they depended on several techniques, the most obvious being a summary verdict based on evidence presented by the contending parties. Such a hearing occurred on May 19, 1852, when Judge José María Martínez attempted to end the recurrent wrangle between Arroyo Hondo and Desmontes over water from the Rio Hondo. After hearing arguments from both sides, Martínez modified the ayuntamiento decree of 1824 by ruling that, although Arroyo Hondo had "preference" in the stream, Desmontes was entitled to one-third of the water, even in times of shortage.[16] In the 1990s, residents of the two communities still disagree as to whether that allocation became sanctioned by custom in later years.

In 1864, Judge Juan Santistevan tackled another touchy issue: division of the Rio Lucero between Arroyo Seco, Fernando de Taos, and Los Estiércoles. Following the armed confrontation at the mouth of the ditch in 1838, the contenders had coexisted reasonably well for a few decades, but trouble erupted again in 1864. When people from Estiércoles shut off the Acequia Madre del Rio

Lucero on June 18, a determined group from Arroyo Seco reopened it with approval from the local juez de paz. Hoping for an equitable settlement, the aggrieved parties turned to Santistevan, who listened to several witnesses and then proposed an allotment based on a sliding scale. When the Lucero carried fifteen surcos, Arroyo Seco received three; when there were ten surcos, the portion dropped to two; if the flow dwindled to eight surcos, Arroyo Seco was allowed only one, but that was to be a guaranteed minimum.[17] Although the judge deserved credit for a good try, his ruling ignored the interests of Taos Pueblo, which had to be considered in any permanent settlement.

## The Jury System and Committees of Experts

Occasionally, prefects impaneled a jury to hear water cases. Jury trials were unknown in New Mexico before the U.S. takeover, but the populace seems to have readily accepted the concept in both civil and criminal cases. When water became scarce in the midst of the irrigation season of 1861, residents of the village of Los Córdovas, represented by Feliz and José Córdova, brought suit against the mayordomos in charge of three acequias originating from the Rio Grande del Rancho. To decide on an equitable division between Los Córdovas and the upstream community of Ranchos de Taos, Judge Pedro Valdez selected twelve "good men and true." After due consideration, the jury ruled that the Los Ranchos mayordomos must give immediate relief to their neighbors below by allowing four surcos of water to run down for four days and nights. After that time, Los Córdovas was to receive one-third of the river's flow, a ruling adopted by the court on July 1.[18]

At other times when prefectos heard a difficult water case, they named a committee of experts to make an investigation and report back to the court—a traditional procedure used frequently in earlier years by Spanish and Mexican officials, as we have seen. Sometimes referred to as *peritos,* the experts were respected community members who had no interest in the issue under consideration. Usually, judges accepted their recommendations without changes. In July 1879, when Los Córdovas reopened the ongoing struggle with Ranchos de Taos, Judge Joseph reviewed the Valdez decision of 1861 and then appointed a three-man commission to give advice. After inspecting the irrigated lands at both settlements, the experts reported that the fields upstream at Los Ranchos were eight times larger than those at Los Córdovas. Because the season had been very dry, they found only four surcos flowing in the river. To assist the downstream farmers during the shortage, they suggested a time schedule that allocated all the water to Los Córdovas from sunset on Friday until sunrise on Sunday.[19] Judge Joseph approved the report and considered the matter closed, but a few days later the Los Ranchos people asked for a rehearing; the investigation, they said, had been too hasty. Amiably, the judge named a new commission for further research. When its members returned, they declared that fields at Los

Ranchos were ten times larger than those below and proposed some adjustments in the distribution schedule. Although Los Córdovas retained the same weekend hours, Los Ranchos received a single surco during that time to be used alternately by acequias on each side of the river. Again, Judge Joseph discharged the commissioners with thanks and adopted their recommendations, thus patching up the quarrel until the next drought.[20]

*Probate Courts*

Although they probably lacked jurisdiction, Taos County courts sometimes attempted to mediate apportionment issues between Hispano irrigators and their Indian counterparts at the pueblo of Taos. As noted above, settlers at Fernando de Taos received authorization from Governor Fernando Chacón to use sobrante water from the Pueblo and Lucero rivers in 1797. For many years, farmers depending on the Rio Pueblo managed to maintain reasonably good relations with the Indians upstream, unlike their counterparts under the Lucero. Evidently, the two groups found ways to share the stream without recourse to lawsuits. Trouble began in 1871, however, when a commission of citizens from Don Fernando complained to Judge Pedro Sánchez that the Pueblos had interfered with the river's flow and prevented them from watering their fields. In a hearing on July 10, the Indians conceded a water right to the complainants, but insisted that the real problem was proper allocation during times of scarcity. Judge Sánchez quickly disposed of the matter by ordering the pueblo to allow a permanent allotment of two surcos for villagers downstream—a hasty decision that proved unsatisfactory.[21]

Seven years later, Hispano irrigators returned to probate court, seeking similar relief. In response, Judge Joseph summoned José María Luján, governor of the pueblo, and other principales to come before him. The Indian leaders managed to elude Sheriff Gabriel Lucero, however, and failed to appear at the appointed time. Undeterred, Joseph established an arbitration committee composed of Luján, Lucero, and the mayordomo of Don Fernando's acequia madre, directing them to meet in the Rio Pueblo canyon above the uppermost pueblo dam. At that point, they were to calculate the number of surcos carried by the river and divide them equally between the Indians and the settlers. On July 11, 1878, Sheriff Lucero reported to Judge Joseph that the court's order had been carried out.[22]

In their courtrooms, probate judges considered other water issues besides apportionment between contending groups of users. Frequently acequia management problems, such as enforcement of work regulations, appeared on court dockets, requiring time and attention. At Las Vegas, in March 1849, Prefect Herman Grolman set forth a set of rules to be observed by mayordomos and landowners throughout San Miguel County. After reminding property holders of their legal obligation to participate in acequia maintenance, Grolman directed the mayordomos to give at least one day's notice before starting cleanup projects. Any parciantes who refused to work could be arraigned in justice courts, where they were subject to fines of one dollar for each day missed. Those fortunate individuals who furnished a cart with oxen would be excused from ordinary labor that day.[23]

Officials in Santa Ana County (now Sandoval County) faced comparable difficulties. At the request of Jesús María Silva y Rivera, mayordomo of the acequia común de Peña Blanca, Probate Judge Tomás C. de Baca promulgated a similar code in March 1871. Under its terms, mayordomos were required to make just and equitable work assignments according to the laws and customs prevailing in the community. All parciantes must take part in acequia mainte- nance, but no individual need work for three days consecutively. Mayordomos had authority to levy the usual fines for malingering but were also responsible for reading the complete list of work rules at the job site so that no one could pretend ignorance. Conscious of their authority, Peña Blanca's mayordomos did not hesitate to chastise miscreants who failed to work when ordered, showed disrespect toward authorities, or diverted water without proper authorization.[24] Under certain conditions, however, dissatisfied water users could refuse to con- tinue maintenance of their ditch and construct a new one. In 1849, a group formerly dominated by Juan Vigil, prominent landowner of Tomé, received authorization from Prefect Santiago Hubbell to end the association and water their fields with a newly built acequia. Vigil was to receive use of the old desagüe "without damage to a third party." Hubbell also ordered the latter to establish and maintain a substantial bridge where the *camino nacional* cut across his ditch, "wide enough for all the carriage traffic of this territory."[25]

One of the reasons mayordomos and county officials insisted on proper acequia maintenance was to minimize the danger of flood damage, a continual headache at many locations. As the county executive, probate judges had re- sponsibility for the upkeep of roads, bridges, and other public facilities. Near the end of 1852, unusually heavy rains combined with uncontrolled waste water from several acequias to form a large lake just north of the plaza at Tomé. Ob- serving that the inundation had caused serious injury to the church and other public buildings, Valencia County's probate judge, José Francisco Castillo, threatened anyone turning additional water toward the lake with a whop- ping fine of twenty-five pesos. To minimize damage, Castillo also ordered the acequia madre's mayordomo to begin an immediate effort to drain the plaza and adjacent streets, imposing a fine of five pesos on any resident refus- ing to help out.[26] In like fashion, in the summer of 1877 carelessness allowed waste water from the Cuchilla ditch at Desmontes to pour over the wagon road running from Taos to Red River, making the usual thoroughfare impass- able. Alerted to the problem by county road inspectors, Judge Joseph demanded prompt corrective action from Juan Emilio Herrera, the mayordomo responsible.[27]

Sometimes engineering changes in particular acequia systems caused controversy that came before probate courts for resolution. When a poorly designed diversion dam on the Rio Pecos flooded lands at San Miguel del Vado in 1866, Judge Antonio Baca y Baca ordered appointment of the usual three-man investigative team. After an on-site inspection, committee members reported that the dam had been built at least one vara too high, unnecessarily forcing the pent-up pond over adjacent fields. As a corrective, they recommended some structural alterations and compensatory damages for the complaining landholders.[28] Some years later, the probate judge of Taos County named a similar advisory commission to relocate a desagüe that provided relief drainage for a principal ditch from the Rio Fernando, La Acequia del Sur del Cañón. The first proposal, that the channel run through the Arroyo de la Cruz Alta, brought such complaints from a few disaffected landowners that Judge Antonio Tercio Gallegos asked a new committee to offer another opinion. When the second report reiterated findings of the first, the court decided to accept it with a few modifications. To mollify the dissenters, Gallegos directed the acequia's mayordomo to place a headgate (*compuerta*) at the former site of the desagüe, thus assuring them a water supply when their turn came to irrigate.[29]

In the spring of 1877, a very unusual water management case, one with environmental implications, came before Judge Joseph. On May 10, Sheriff Gabriel Lucero and twenty other landowners, who depended on the Rio Fernando for irrigation water, complained that a certain Juan Sánchez had been systematically cutting down large numbers of cottonwood trees near the river's headwaters. In so doing, Sánchez and his employees eliminated the cooling shade that protected the stream. According to the petitioners, exposure to the blazing summer sun would cause water shortages from evaporation, bringing hardships for all concerned. After ordering an appearance by Sánchez, Judge Joseph ruled in favor of the plaintiffs, finding that excessive timber cutting in the bosque would lead, little by little, to diminution of the water so necessary for agriculture in the valley. Thereafter, anyone convicted of such destruction would be regarded as a transgressor, subject to all the rigors of the law.[30] Although nineteenth-century New Mexicans generally seemed unaware of environmental issues, Joseph's ruling marks a significant exception.

Obviously, probate courts exercised great power in county affairs and provided a convenient forum for resolution of local problems, including water administration. Because Hispanos maintained large electoral majorities during the first decades of territorial government, they almost always selected one of their own for the important office of probate judge. Exercising powers conferred to them by the Kearny Code and Organic Act, the judges, in turn, managed to

preserve time-honored procedures for settling water issues within their jurisdictions. To resolve apportionment disputes, judges frequently relied on fact-
finding committees of disinterested citizens—a recognized practice. Water allocations among contending groups were usually expressed in time schedules
or in customary measurements, such as surcos—procedures with deep communal roots. Although judicial rulings seldom pleased all interested parties, they
usually represented a sensible compromise based on tradition and common
sense rather than strict adherence to the law.

*The Legislature*

To complement decisions rendered in probate courts, New Mexicans made
use of the territorial legislature to preserve conventional forms of water administration. As in the local court system, Hispanos dominated the legislative
branch for several decades, retaining control of both the council and the house.
During the first session in July 1851, lawmakers began to codify old practices
derived from Spanish law and custom, writing them into statutes for the new
territory. The first act passed authorized citizens to construct acequias as
needed and take water for them "wherever they can," paying just compensation
for right-of-way. Other sections prohibited construction of any impediment
to irrigation and mandated labor obligations for owners of lands adjoining
ditches. In the second session six months later, legislators enacted a bill specifying responsibilities of mayordomos, procedures for their election, and causes
for their removal from office in case of neglect of duty.[31] Throughout the process,
lawmakers reaffirmed two important principles from the past: the primacy of
agriculture in water allocation and establishment of the community acequia as
the preeminent institution for water governance.[32]

In addition to general laws that effected the entire territory, legislators frequently passed special bills intended to resolve local problems. At times, such
laws provided the extra authority needed to deal with an emergency situation,
but often their passage suggests that regular procedures had failed, causing litigants to seek legislative intervention as a last resort. Measures adopted for flood
control are good examples of the first category. In 1865, heavy spring rains and
melting snows brought the Rio Grande out of its banks, causing widespread
devastation all the way from Taos to Las Cruces. In the Albuquerque area, rising
water forced several plazas, Atrisco, Pajarito, and Los Padillas, to be temporarily
abandoned.[33] In January, during the next session, legislators enacted two bills,
one for each side of the river, intended to prevent a similar catastrophe by mo-
bilizing Albuquerque's citizens well in advance of the spring runoff. With oversight from the probate judge, juezes de paz at the endangered villages received
authorization to collect cash contributions and enlist all able-bodied males for
construction of a series of levees made with brush and sod. Labor was to be
pro-rated according to property ownership, but assignments could be mitigated

by monetary donations. Individuals tapped for duty by the overseers in charge were subject to fines of two dollars per day for failure to appear.[34]

Although less threatened from inundation by the Rio Grande, Taos residents also suffered serious flood damage from time to time. Like their Bernalillo County colleagues, house and council members from Taos pushed special legislation to organize their constituents for preventative action. Anticipating serious problems near the junction of the Rio Lucero and the Rio Pueblo in the spring of 1869, the legislature passed a law on February 7 calling for election of a special mayordomo by landowners in the endangered area. Responsible for erecting a network of dams (*atarques*) and dikes (*estacados*) to protect farmlands where the streams met, the mayordomo could order neighborhood residents to participate or face substantial fines.[35] In each of these instances, elected representatives exercised legislative powers to safeguard interests of the community during emergencies.

The legislature manifested a similar concern for the general welfare by initiating public works projects at several locations to secure community water supplies for agricultural and domestic purposes. In 1869, population growth at Las Cruces necessitated construction of a large lateral from the town's acequia madre to irrigate farmlands recently put into production. A bill enacted in January confirmed the route selected by three commissioners for this important ditch. Beginning north of the plaza, it ran south down the main street, east of the church, returning to the acequia madre near Numa Grandjean's gristmill. The latter ditch, which originated from the Rio Grande near Doña Ana, had to be widened sufficiently to carry the increased flow. Once again, the act required that all adult males from eighteen to sixty contribute their labor, although the lawmakers hoped that enough funds could be raised from voluntary subscriptions to pay for bridges needed at street crossings.[36]

Several years later, representatives from San Miguel County proposed an innovative scheme to develop some potentially rich farmlands about ten miles north of Las Vegas, which had remained unused for lack of irrigation water. Later known as Ten Lakes, the area included a number of natural reservoirs adjoining the Rio Sapelló near the villages of Los Alamos and Joya Larga. Observing a potential for additional storage at the lakes, the bill's promoters contemplated construction of canals to carry the river's surplus into them, with other acequias conveying accumulated supplies from their outlets for use at the farmsteads. Only those landowners who participated in excavating the channels obtained rights to the stored water. To protect users already depending on the Sapelló, the law stipulated that no diversions to the lakes take place except when surpluses became available or during winter.[37]

Across the Sangre de Cristo range to the west, city fathers in Santa Fe considered ways to augment the municipal water supply as an accommodation for farmers and a growing urban population. On January 24, 1861, the legislature passed a bill ordering the county's probate judge to appoint three commissioners, "men of learning and science," to study the feasibility of introducing water from the Pecos drainage, over the mountains east of town, into the headwaters of the Rio Santa Fe. Nothing came of that proposal because of engineering problems and strong opposition from Pecoseños, which forced lawmakers to try a new approach. Four years later, they enacted another bill authorizing construction of a large dam made of "solid masonry, stone and mortar" to impound water from the Santa Fe River during times of surplus. As usual, commissioners in charge of the project were instructed to open a subscription list, but, if voluntary donations fell short, they also had authorization to spend tax money of an unspecified amount. Again, the bill's authors expected local citizens to contribute their labor without pay.[38] Despite the provision for tax support, proponents of Santa Fe's dam lacked financing, which forced its postponement for another two decades.

## New Approaches to Apportionment

Besides coping with emergencies and initiating public works, territorial legislators also enacted laws to settle local water disputes. Statutes enacted for such purposes suggest that usual procedures for conflict resolution had broken down, causing aggrieved parties to seek redress through legislative action. South of Taos, for example, equitable distribution of water from the Rio Grande del Rancho between Los Ranchos and Los Córdovas continued to be a festering issue despite probate court decisions in 1861 and 1879. Attempting a more forceful approach, the legislature passed an act on February 7, 1882 that declared the Rio Grande del Rancho an acequia madre to be used by the two placitas without preference for either. In times of scarcity, juezes de paz and mayordomos from each community were authorized to meet and arrange a just allotment of the available flow *"without appeal or recourse"* (emphasis added).[39] Similarly, lawmakers enacted a bill in 1865 to end a quarrel between citizens of La Mesa and Santo Tomás in Doña Ana County. Under its terms, La Mesa obtained a free right to irrigate with waste water turned into the desagüe of Santo Tomás without having to perform any maintenance work in return. Parciantes from the latter village retained a superior priority, however, and were not obligated to open their desagüe, even when La Mesa's ditch had no water at its intake.[40] Another law passed in 1876 provided that landowners in Bernalillo County at Rancho de San Mateo, who had recently lost their headgate to floods, might share part of the ditch serving Corrales, if they performed a proportionate share of the necessary maintenance.[41]

During sessions at Santa Fe, New Mexico's legislators devoted themselves to questions of proper land and water use from time to time. In the early 1860s, a population influx at Las Truchas vexed long-time residents, who derived their land titles from the original grantees, convincing representatives from Rio Arriba County to support remedial legislation. On January 18, 1865, they passed a bill forbidding anyone from taking possession of land above the area previously under cultivation for farming or house construction. Encroachment harmed the old families by reducing the commons used for pasture and curtailing their supply of irrigation water.[42] Several years later, settlers near Rayado, in Mora County, pushed legislation to solve a water distribution problem. As drafted, the act declared the Agua Dulce to be a public stream, free for irrigation by all. Farmland had priority, however; diversion into vegas for hay production was not allowed.[43] But such regulations were not always uniform throughout the territory. When the same issue arose in Rio Arriba County in 1880, lawmakers declared grass cultivation to be worthy of protection and encouragement. While conceding that farmlands enjoyed preference, they required mayordomos in their county to provide water for meadows.[44]

On rare occasions, lawmakers also took steps to preserve water quality, notably in an effort to clean up Socorro's domestic supply in 1871. Expressing dismay that washerwomen had been plying their trade in the town's acequia madre, which ran from mountain springs to the plaza, the legislature prohibited all laundering or bathing in the ditch. Violators could expect fines ranging from five to twenty-five dollars, but filling tubs from the acequia was still allowed. As a further corrective, the bill imposed similar fines on those who allowed hogs to roam at will and wallow in the acequia's muddy bottom; it also prevented, without express permission from the mayordomo, diversion of water from the acequia madre until it had passed the town's several gristmills—a more prosaic afterthought.[45]

## Local Action

Frequently, New Mexicans resolved water problems without recourse to governmental institutions, depending instead on time-honored practices, such as community meetings or arbitration by impartial advisers. At times, the opposing parties worked hard to reach a compromise as a way of avoiding the expense of litigation. Near Taos in 1856, for example, parciantes from the Revalse and Desmontes acequias, which both depended on the Rio Hondo, appointed *juezes árbitros* to reconcile an apportionment dispute, thus eliminating "the immense costs arising from a lawsuit." After some discussion, the two juezes, Padre Antonio José Martínez and his foster son, Santiago Valdés, proposed an irrevocable allotment of three surcos for the Revalse, subject to some modification during extreme drought. The parties agreed that disinterested persons, who understood the exact size of a surco, would make the first measurement and then chisel an indelible mark at the Revalse's intake so that the amount could not be changed without detection. In return, the acequia's users promised never to enlarge or lengthen their ditch in the future. When the compact had been signed, the adversaries received copies and filed the original with the clerk of the territorial district court.[46]

In the previous example, the juezes árbitros made a division based on volume, but sometimes a time schedule seemed preferable. In 1853, changes in land ownership along the Cañada Miranda above Ranchos de Taos caused the proprietors to reapportion water from some hot springs that irrigated their valley. Now known inappropriately as Ponce de León Hot Springs, the water source had been divided during the Mexican period by Maurilo Bargas and Pedro Martín, the earliest settlers, who claimed exclusive rights in rotation for fifteen days and eight days respectively. Those two had conceded an equal right to Tomás Fernández for an unstated period. Subsequently, a Francisco Gonzales had purchased Martín's property; and Gonzales and his brothers had bought the Fernández lands and part of those belonging to Maurilo Bargas. Rumaldo Bargas owned the rest. Under the new arrangement planned by Rumaldo and Francisco Gonzales, Bargas received the springs' flow for nine days, Gonzales and his brothers for nine days, and Gonzales for four days. In a spirit of neighborliness, the principals announced an intention to help each other with loans of water whenever necessary during their respective periods. At the same time, they conceded a very tenuous sobrante right as an act of kindness to thirteen individuals who collectively farmed a small parcel (*laborcita*) on the plain below. Stipulating that the beneficiaries not break out the tiniest bit of new land, Bargas and Gonzales appointed themselves joint mayordomos with full control of water distribution for the hot springs.[47] The concern demonstrated by the landowners for each other's difficulties and for the unfortunates downstream demonstrates a strong sense of community responsibility.

When shortages threatened, contending groups sometimes found ways to iron out their differences during public meetings, such as the one convened at Taos County Courthouse on August 2, 1893. Led by Taos Pueblo's Governor Domingo Bernal, thirteen *principales* met with Juan Santistevan and five other representatives of Taos town to reapportion the Rio Pueblo. Following the settlement reached in Judge Joseph's courtroom fifteen years earlier, the stream had been free from serious controversy, but dry weather and increased use necessitated a new division. Shifting from the measured allotment mandated by Joseph, the negotiators set up a schedule for times of scarcity that gave Fernando de Taos the user's entire flow from twilight Friday until dawn Monday. Next, irrigators under the acequia madre, including those near the cemetery, had exclusive use of the water all day Monday. At other times, the stream belonged to the Indians, giving them complete control for about four days a week. After the meeting, the signatories proceeded to the county clerk's office to record what they had done.[48]

As the rural population grew, communities sometimes organized meetings to consider the pros and cons of extending their acequias to irrigate additional lands. Although the new fields probably belonged to relatives of neighboring ditch owners, the subject required serious deliberation. In January 1882, dueños of Belén's acequia madre appointed a board of commissioners to negotiate with sixteen residents of nearby Jarales who had petitioned for use of their ditch. After lengthy talks, the two groups reached a ten-point agreement not unlike the one hammered out in 1829 at Desmontes and discussed in chapter 3. Under its terms, the petitioners promised to build and maintain their own contracequia, or lateral ditch, which began at the mill of the deceased Antonio Chaves and followed a very specific route determined by the commissioners. Work assignments (*tasos*), as determined by the acequia madre's mayordomo, would be performed by everyone together, with no excuses for noncompliance. During the first year, the newcomers were required to contribute an extra twenty days of labor in the ditch as a kind of initiation fee. If, in the future, other landowners asked to use the ditch, the sixteen would not be allowed to vote in their favor. Finally, the supplicants assumed the costs of registering the agreement with county officials.[49]

Other settlements of the same kind were much simpler than the one arranged between Belén and Jarales. At El Rito Colorado, a tiny placita below Laguna pueblo on the Rio San José, nineteen parciantes of the village acequia madre signed their names to a document in 1888 that allowed Federico Luna a right to sobrante water from their ditch. In return, Luna paid out a single peso (in U.S. currency) and promised to provide a peón for the annual spring work detail.[50] A similar situation prevailed near Taos between Manuel Andrés Trujillo and owners of the Revalse acequia, which carries water from the Rio Hondo across the Desmontes plain before wasting into Arroyo Seco. During the Mexican era, Trujillo had obtained authorization to use the Revalse's sobrante for irrigation of lands below the junction near Las Colonias, a right confirmed in 1849 by Charles Beaubien, district judge in New Mexico's newly established court system. In 1871, owners of the Revalse composed a carefully worded statement to clarify relations between the two parties. For more than thirty years, they declared, Trujillo had used the excess from their acequia without troubling them in any way. Therefore, they granted to him, his heirs, and successors, a perpetual right to surplus waters that became available from the Revalse without damage to their own irrigation, but no more—a cautious reaffirmation of Trujillo's prerogative.[51]

Public meetings also provided a forum to determine appropriate locations for gristmills—a matter that often caused difficult water problems. On April 17, 1855, settlers north of Mora on the Guadalupita Grant convened to decide if Felipe Baca, a fellow citizen, might set up such an enterprise within the *pisos comunes*, an area set aside for mills, threshing, grazing, and other communal activities when the grant was made. During the meeting, Baca received the necessary authorization by agreeing to build a bridge over the millrace strong enough for carts. He promised to forego compensation if stray livestock caused cave-ins along his ditch banks and he also obligated himself to pay for any animals killed or injured near the mill by his family, servants, or dogs.[52]

Usually, mill owners secured right-of-way privileges more easily by making small cash payments to neighboring property owners.[53] Under certain circumstances, however, transactions of that kind became more complex. In 1864, Ramón Ortega and two associates sold their rights to a part of the acequia madre at Barelas below Albuquerque for one hundred pesos to a group of parciantes in the same ditch headed by the mayordomo, Gregorio Barela. Declaring his portion to be public (*común*) henceforth, Ortega also received exclusive rights to all the acequia's sobrante for his gristmill and was relieved of any responsibility for future damages incurred.[54] Certainly, Barela and his compadres must have sorely needed Ortega's ditch to offer him such an advantageous contract. Five years later, Ortega sold his sobrante rights for an undisclosed sum to Ambrosio Armijo, one of Albuquerque's great *ricos* during the late nineteenth century.

From the previous discussion, it is evident that New Mexicans managed to shape the institutions imposed by territorial government so that they became compatible with traditional forms of water management. In doing so, they continued to address the same problems that had troubled officials during Spanish and Mexican administrations: equitable apportionment, labor obligations, damages resulting from spillage, and flood control.

Clearly, apportionment continued to be the most difficult issue. During the early territorial period, procedures to resolve such controversies frequently failed. It must be remembered, however, that in some cases a permanent settlement was impossible because demand for water greatly exceeded the supply available in dry years. Despite serious shortcomings, the interim measures imposed locally allowed contending groups to share the shortage until changing climatic conditions brought increased stream flow. Although the process seldom pleased everyone, it afforded a high level of community participation. With few exceptions, decisions reached by probate judges, legislative acts, and ad hoc agreements arranged publicly or privately reflected traditional values and time-honored procedures for water management.

# 5 | Water Administration in New Mexico During the Late Territorial Era

O N  A  CHILLY afternoon in December 1888, an unusual group of passengers climbed down from the Denver & Rio Grande Railway's southbound train at Embudo, a tiny station on the Rio Grande forty miles north of Santa Fe. Conspicuous in their Eastern attire, the eight new arrivals were all recent graduates of prestigious engineering schools: they had traveled to Embudo to learn a technique of water measurement known as stream gauging. Responding to a sudden increased interest in Western irrigation, Congress had passed a joint resolution in March authorizing the Secretary of Interior to examine potential irrigated lands, locate possible sites for water storage, and determine the capacity of various streams.[1]

Responsibility for the project fell to John Wesley Powell, heroic explorer of the Colorado River, then serving as director of the United States Geological Survey. Many considered Powell to be "the father of irrigation development in the American West."[2] Recognizing a shortage of personnel trained in water measurement, Powell ordered his protégé, Frederick Haynes Newell, to establish a school for hydrographers on a Western river. Embudo was selected because of its situation in an arid region on a major stream unlikely to freeze in winter. For the next five months, Newell's class made regular measurements of water temperature, depth, and velocity in the Rio Grande from a makeshift raft anchored above their camp. When classes ended in April 1889, the engineers scattered to assume positions as hydrographers throughout the West.[3] Introducing new scientific procedures and advanced technology, Newell's school exemplified the changes that increasingly characterized irrigation in New Mexico at the end of the nineteenth century.

With his work at Embudo completed, Newell wrote two important reports on irrigation for the U.S. Geological Survey and the Bureau of the Census—reports that included his views on conditions in New Mexico. A native of western Pennsylvania and a graduate of the Massachusetts Institute of Technology, the young engineer had had only limited experience in the West. Like many Easterners, he reacted to New Mexicans and their irrigation practices with a mixture of opprobrium and wonder.

Observing that agricultural production was relatively low, Newell concluded that the average farmer, "especially [one] of Spanish and Indian descent," demonstrated little skill or energy, which resulted in small returns for his efforts. Misunderstanding the local culture, he attributed the "lack of industry" to indifference for the future and, more significantly, continual uncertainty as to the water supply for irrigation.[4] During his travels, Newell never ceased to marvel at the antiquity of the acequias, particularly in the Rio Grande Valley, where he noted that Indians and Spaniards still used the original ditches and that few changes had occurred "within the memory of man." In almost every region, he criticized the large number of small acequias, each with its own flimsy diversion dam, remarking that one or two well-designed "high-line canals" would function more efficiently and irrigate a much greater acreage.[5] On the other hand, Newell grudgingly approved of the community acequia system in which each farmer paid his "water tax" by working on the acequia annually, and control of the water remained in the hands of the irrigators.[6]

In his reports, Newell also discussed the first large-scale, capital-intensive water projects recently constructed in New Mexico, which contrasted sharply with the traditional Hispano community ditch systems. Entranced by the economic possibilities resulting from massive development, politicians and entrepreneurs from every Western state and territory regarded irrigation as the key to future growth. New Mexico was no exception. In Colfax County, on the famed Maxwell Land Grant, Newell found substantial acreage watered by enormous canals from Cimarron and Vermejo creeks. Scooped out by a battalion of horse-drawn scrapers, each ditch was twenty feet wide at the bottom and ten or twelve miles long.[7] To the southeast, on the Rio Pecos, the Pecos Valley Irrigation and Improvement Company had dug a huge channel near Roswell, and seventy miles downstream at Eddy (present Carlsbad), the same corporation was building an even bigger project. Contractors had erected a limestone dam, 40 feet high and 1,100 feet long, that backed up the Pecos more than seven miles. When all the dams, flumes, canals, and laterals were completed, the system would irrigate lands on both sides of the river all the way to the Texas border.[8] Certainly, New Mexico had never before seen water projects of such magnitude, but this was just the beginning. Although much more restrained than most observers, Newell envisioned similar projects on the San Juan, in the Taos Valley, and along the lower Rio Grande. He recognized the dangers of overdevelopment, however, and deplored the unrestrained expansion in Colorado's San Luis Valley that had caused great hardship and uncertainty for New Mexico's farmers downstream.[9]

As described by Newell in 1890, New Mexico had changed greatly since becoming a territory forty years earlier. During that period, the population had grown steadily, rising from 60,000 in 1850 to more than 90,000 ten years later—a gain of 50 percent (see table 1). Although a number of soldiers, traders, and other Anglo-Americans had arrived as immigrants, most of the expansion came

Table 1. Population of New Mexico, 1850–1910[12]

| Year | Population | Percent of Increase |
|------|-----------|---------------------|
| 1850 | 41,547 | |
| 1860 | 93,516 | 51.9 |
| 1870 | 91,874 | (1.8) |
| 1880 | 119,565 | 30.1 |
| 1890 | 160,282 | 34.1 |
| 1900 | 195,310 | 21.9 |
| 1910 | 327,301 | 67.6 |

from natural increase of the native population.[10] No growth occurred during the 1860s, but from 1870 to 1890 New Mexico's population soared to 160,000 persons, and then more than doubled in the next twenty years, reaching 327,000 by 1910. After the arrival of the railroad in December 1878, immigration grew steadily. According to the census of 1910, 40 percent of New Mexico's citizenry had been born in other states.[11]

*The Effects of Rail Transport*

Without doubt, population growth in the territory was greatly enhanced by the arrival of rail transportation at the end of 1878. During the fall, contractors employed by the Atchison, Topeka and Santa Fe Railway had graded a roadbed and laid tracks over Raton Pass from Trinidad, Colorado. On December 7, the first locomotive crossed the pass, as crews of laborers pushed the line further south.[13] When the rails reached Lamy, slightly more than a year later, New Mexico's legislature passed a joint resolution declaring "this event . . . as the most important in the history of the territory." According to historian Ralph Emerson Twitchell, arrival of the Santa Fe and its rivals marked "the beginning of an era of permanent prosperity" in which the people awakened to "the enlightened progress and modern methods . . . of the eastern states."[14] Such hyperbole exemplified the spirit of the times, but cheap transportation did serve to stimulate local businesses and integrate New Mexico into the national economy for the first time.

As other railroads began to compete with the Santa Fe, they encouraged immigration, both domestic and foreign, bringing new citizens with valuable skills and capital for investment. Between 1880 and 1890, property valuations more than quadrupled, rising from $49 million to $231 million.[15] Recognizing opportunity, entrepreneurs soon appeared to seek profits and prestige from ventures in mining, cattle ranching, and irrigated lands.

## Powell and the Introduction of Large-Scale Irrigation

The entry of railroads into New Mexico coincided neatly with a sudden surge of interest in irrigation as a means of "reclaiming" arid lands for agriculture. In 1878, John Wesley Powell, then an Interior Department employee, presented his famous *Report on the Lands of the Arid Regions of the United States,* "one of the most important books ever to come out of the West," according to an eminent historian.[16] A national hero after his daring exploration of the Colorado River, Powell had become an expert on Western land and water issues. In the report and in other writings and speeches, he discussed the feasibility of bringing irrigation to immense portions of the public domain. As a preliminary, he proposed a general survey of Western lands to determine areas best suited for reclamation and an inventory of appropriate sites for large-scale water storage. To prevent monopolization of water resources by special interests, he advocated an entirely new system for allocation of public lands in subhumid regions. Recognizing that many lesser streams had already been preempted, Powell called for cooperative developments on major water courses, financed jointly by the nation's "great capitalists" with state and/or federal assistance. Because his radical ideas threatened those who benefitted from the status quo, Powell's proposals aroused powerful opposition from Western businessmen and politicians. Nevertheless, after ten years of debate, Congress approved the survey and put Powell in charge.[17]

As irrigation excitement grew in New Mexico, politicos of every persuasion hurriedly embraced grandiose water projects with almost hysterical enthusiasm. In his annual report of 1887 to the Secretary of the Interior, Governor Edmund G. Ross, a Democrat, declared that more than half of the territory's 78 million acres could be turned into productive farmland through development of reliable water supplies.[18] An Ohio native, Ross envisioned New Mexico as a land dotted with small, productive homesteads like those found in the Midwest. His political rivals, who agreed with him on little else, expressed similar opinions. Testifying before a U.S. Senate committee in 1890, Thomas B. Catron, doyen of the Republican Party, urged a survey of water resources, declaring that the New Mexico territory possessed no less than 150 streams suitable for storage projects. Similarly, territorial secretary William G. Ritch stated that irrigated acreage could easily be enlarged forty or fifty times over, reaching even the most remote areas by means of pipes.

Other boosters touted possibilities in their own localities. Albert J. Fountain, a prominent attorney from La Mesilla, suggested that up to ten million acres east of the Rio Grande on the fearsome Jornada del Muerto might be brought under cultivation for such exotic crops as rice, tobacco, and cotton. Millions more awaited the plow in Doña Ana County and, to the east, across the San Andrés Mountains in the Tularosa basin. More conservatively, future governor Miguel Otero predicted that an additional three or four hundred thousand acres would soon be developed near Albuquerque.[19] Based on estimates of arable lands rather than available water supplies, all these projections proved to be highly inflated.

Perceiving the tremendous potential for economic growth presented by large water projects, the territorial legislature established new institutions to facilitate development. On February 24, 1887, lawmakers passed a bill authorizing incorporation of irrigation companies as a means of providing the capital resources needed for major construction. Under its terms, any five or more persons desiring to construct and maintain reservoirs, canals, ditches, or pipelines for irrigation purposes could draw up a corporate charter to be registered with the territorial secretary. In addition to demonstrating financial responsibility, such companies were required to specify the points of beginning and ending of major canals and their general direction. They were allowed to enter private property for the purpose of making surveys, to exercise the right of eminent domain for acquisition of right-of-way, and to divert *surplus* (emphasis added) waters from any stream, lake, or spring in the territory. To safeguard existing users, the legislators also established some important restrictions. Water companies could not make diversions interfering with the needs of prior appropriations, nor could they take water required by a public acequia between February 15 and October 15 without the unanimous consent of every agricultural landowner under the ditch.[20] By superimposing new legislation on the old, territorial lawmakers attempted, simultaneously, to accommodate innovative irrigation technology and to preserve and protect the community acequia, traditionally the foundation for water administration in New Mexico. In effect, they created a dualistic authority intended to bridge the gap between the past and the future. Although successful in many ways, their efforts sometimes led to conflicts when the two systems came together.

## Changes in the Pattern of Litigation

### Local Control Is Diminished

During the 1880s, important changes also occurred in the procedures for settling water disputes. With increasing frequency, water cases were litigated in territorial district courts instead of county probate courts, which brought a diminution of local control. For many years, district judges had resented the political influence enjoyed by the local judiciary and were eager to see their wings clipped. In 1876, the legislature passed an act establishing a three-man board of commissioners for each county that assumed many of the powers previously exercised by probate judges for county administration and supervision of elections.[21] Although the legislature did not enact any specific bills giving district judges jurisdiction over water issues, litigants increasingly sought relief in their chambers.

At the precinct level, justices of the peace continued to hear cases of lesser importance. By 1897, jurisdiction of probate courts had been largely confined to wills and testaments, estate administration, guardianship of minors, and similar matters.[22] Significant consequences resulted from the shift into district court, including a new dependence on attorneys, more formalized procedures, and greater emphasis on abstract legal principles in reaching decisions. Previously, local officials had been more concerned with finding pragmatic solutions in keeping with community values. Unlike probate judges who were usually members of the Hispano elite, district judges were almost always federal appointees from outside the territory, with limited knowledge of water administration in New Mexico.[23]

Not infrequently, district court dockets included water cases that previous authorities had found difficult to resolve, such as the long-standing quarrel for the Rio Lucero that ranged the pueblo of Taos and Los Estiércoles against Arroyo Seco. Although the division imposed in 1864 by Judge Santistevan had cooled the controversy for two decades, it flared again in 1887. Angered by Arroyo Seco's continuing overappropriation, the Indians closed off the village acequia madre, with encouragement from their agent in Santa Fe. When questioned by a delegation of Hispano farmers, Pueblo Indian leaders replied that, henceforth, their adversaries would be restricted to the old allotment determined by the ayuntamiento in 1824: a single surco measured through the hub of a cartwheel. Since compromise seemed impossible, sixty-seven Arroyo Seco citizens filed suit in district court, requesting an injunction to prevent further interference in their acequia and to force the reopening of a road up Lucero Canyon used by the villagers for cutting timber and firewood. Once begun, the case moved slowly through district court, as both sides changed attorneys, filed motions, and awaited a report prepared by a special master. Finally, on May 13, 1893, after six years of litigation, Judge Edward P. Seeds rendered a verdict favoring the pueblo in which he dismissed the complainants' bill and ordered them to pay the defendants' court costs.[24]

Because 1893 was a dry year, Judge Seed's decision caused an immediate reaction. When mayordomos from the three communities failed to agree on an equitable apportionment of the Lucero's waters, about eighty residents from Taos Pueblo and Los Estiércoles, which had become known as El Prado, proceeded in a body to the intake of the acequia madre where they again shut off its flow. Undaunted by their recent rebuff in court, the people of Arroyo Seco initiated a new lawsuit on July 6, seeking "the right to the waters flowing in the Rio Lucero." In a fine example of courtroom rhetoric, the plaintiffs "prayed" that "the said defendants and every one of them be barred and forever estopped from interfering, diverting, or obstructing the waters in the said river and in the said ditch, or from having any right or title therein, and that your orator's title therein be forever quieted and set at rest." To support that demand, Arroyo Seco relied heavily on confirmation in 1892 by the Court of Private Land Claims of the Antonio Martínez Grant, which included the community's irrigated fields and the disputed ditch.[25] Otherwise, testimony from both sides differed little from that presented during the earlier case.

Eager for a final resolution, Judge James O'Brien, acting temporarily for Judge Seeds, appointed Taos merchant Alexander Gusdorf and Juan Santistevan, the former probate judge, to a three-man commission empowered to divide the stream permanently. In turn, the first two named the last member, William L. McClure, who served as umpire. Less than two weeks after organizing, the commission submitted its report to the court. On July 31, 1893, Judge Seeds, who had returned to the bench, accepted the commission's findings and issued a famous decision. Under its terms, Arroyo Seco received 30 percent of the Lucero's flow, while El Prado and the pueblo of Taos secured 35 percent each; any remaining surplus went to the small intermediate settlement of Las Colonias (Arroyo Seco Abajo).[26]

As examples of water litigation in territorial district courts, the Rio Lucero cases present some interesting points. First, although the opposing parties were all Hispanos or Pueblo Indians, the judges, attorneys, and other responsible officials were almost all Anglos, familiar with the complexities of English common law and the rituals of courtroom procedure. Those with the most at stake participated only as witnesses. Despite that tilt, the proceedings did have some familiar characteristics from earlier times, particularly the reliance on local "experts" to investigate and determine the proper allocation, a common practice under Spanish colonial and Mexican administration. In their report to the court, the three commissioners divided the stream into exact percentages, instead of establishing a time schedule or quantification in traditional units such as surcos. Since water measurement was still an inexact science in New Mexico, the apportionment presented some problems of implementation, requiring construction of a special box, or weir. In recent years, the Seeds decision has been modified somewhat by other lawsuits, but it still endures as a legal landmark.

Apportionment issues such as those that divided irrigators on the Rio Lucero seem to have been particularly troublesome in the Taos Valley, an area in which the several snow-fed mountain streams often proved inadequate for the cultivated acreage under them in dry years. Most disputes proved easier to resolve than the long struggle for the Lucero, however. In 1883, for example, several farmers who irrigated from the Rio Fernando filed suit in district court against three Martínez brothers, Leandro, Agapito, and Severino, charging unlawful preemption of the river's flow through a newly built acequia. In a lengthy complaint, the plaintiffs asserted that they farmed several hundred acres south of the Fernando watered by the Acequia de los Alamitos, which was more than fifty years old. Above their intake, most of the river was turned into a public ditch called the Doña María Dolores Córdova. Between the two headgates, some large springs rose in the riverbed, supplementing the Fernando's meager supply. Previously, the defendants had irrigated with a lateral from the Córdova ditch, but recently they had taken out a new acequia that appropriated the spring's flow—water that the plaintiffs claimed by prior right.

Rising to the challenge, the Martínez brothers responded that they, too, cultivated several hundred acres along the Fernando, lands that had been irrigated for more than seventy years, much longer than those owned by the plaintiffs. As for the so-called new ditch, they claimed that it had been long known as the Acequia de los Martínez, and had been in continual use until the previous year when floods had destroyed their dam. Hence, the work performed had been merely routine repairs, not new construction as charged.

After considering both statements, Judge Samuel B. Axtell took the case under advisement and appointed a Las Cruces attorney, Joseph F. Bonham, to conduct hearings for the court as a "special examiner." A parade of citizens from the Upper Ranchitos community appeared to testify, presenting an array of statements that were often confusing and contradictory. As a result, Judge Axtell sidestepped the priority question in rendering his decision. Instead, he arranged a compromise between the opposing attorneys that recognized the Acequia de los Martínez as a permanent ditch with a water right to be taken out of the Fernando below the Doña María Dolores Córdova ditch. For six days of each month, the first, second, eleventh, twelfth, twenty-first, and twenty-second, the acequia was allowed to run at full capacity, with the proviso that the main stream remain unobstructed on all other days. Both sides agreed to share the court costs equally, including $150 for the special examiner.[27]

In similar fashion, the court agreed to apportion the waters from Lobo Creek, a small tributary of the Rio Hondo, in response to a complaint made in 1896 by Linton M. Cutter against five of his neighbors. To make a reasonable division during the crucial months of June, July, and August, Judge Napoleon B. Laughlin named T. D. Martin and A. G. Müller as arbitrators. After reviewing the evidence, the latter recommended a week-long schedule that gave each of the six parciantes a turn in keeping with his land holdings:[28]

| | |
|---|---|
| L. M. Cutter | 6 A.M. Monday—6 A.M. Wednesday |
| J. C. Spielman | 6 A.M. Wednesday—6 A.M. Friday |
| J. R. Chambers | 6 A.M. Friday—6 A.M. Saturday |
| J. P. Wright | 6 A.M. Saturday—6 A.M. Sunday |
| José Pablo Archuleta | 6 A.M. Sunday—6 P.M. Sunday |
| Juan B. Martínez | 6 P.M. Sunday—6 A.M. Monday |

In each of the preceding cases, the court ignored questions of priority or quantification, opting instead for allotment in units of time, an equitable procedure well known to New Mexican water users.

A different situation arose some years later when Alexander Gusdorf, the merchant who had served as commissioner in the Lucero apportionment, appealed to the court for additional irrigation water from the Rio Chiquito. Hoping to turn a profit from commercial agriculture, Gusdorf wished to seed 800 acres to alfalfa for livestock feed if he could be assured of water to which he was entitled. Although he had owned almost half the land under the Acequia del Llano for more than twenty years and always fulfilled his labor obligations, his neighbors had been unenthusiastic about additional use, forcing him to file suit against the two mayordomos, Juan de Dios Romero and Vidal Gurulé. Claiming a right to not less than one-fourth of the river, he asked the court to grant him the ditch's total capacity one day a week, or two surcos every day during the irrigation season. As a defense, attorneys for the acequia relied on a legal technicality. Under New Mexico law, they argued, the acequia's commissioners should have been named as defendants because they had responsibility for water distribution and they had never refused the plaintiff. Eventually, Gusdorf requested that the suit be dismissed, suggesting a compromise of some sort.[29] However, the case demonstrates a growing interest in acquisition of water rights for ambitious agricultural projects, even in relatively remote areas such as the Taos Valley.

## Diversion Issues and Questions of Precedent

As in the colonial and Mexican eras, lawsuits concerning illegal preemption of irrigation water frequently made their way into district court. Some were easy to resolve, such as the complaint brought by Louis Huning against Adolfo Chávez and Patrocino Córdova in 1899. A businessman and entrepreneur of German descent, Huning had operated a flour mill on a private ditch near Belén for twenty-five years. Always alert to profit opportunities, he had sold the acequia's sobrante as it ran out of the mill for $200 to the community of Los Pueblitos downstream. Unauthorized diversions by Chávez and Córdova, who farmed between the mill and Huning's clients, prevented fulfillment of the contract, forcing him to seek relief in court. When the defendants failed to answer the charges, Judge Jonathan W. Crumpacker issued an injunction barring them from further interference, as requested.[30]

Often diversion issues proved much more complex. In 1887, Esquipula Rodríguez of Las Truchas filed a petition in Rio Arriba County district court declaring that the village mayordomo, José Dolores López, had denied him water. Furthermore, López had neglected his duty as mayordomo by failing to require the plaintiff to participate in the annual ditch cleaning, thus implying that Rodríguez held no interest therein. Threatened with withering crops, he prayed the court for a writ of mandamus forcing López to recognize his rights. In response, the mayordomo painted a different picture. Rodríguez, he said, had sold his property near the village and was squatting on a large tract of commons within the grant west of the road to Las Trampas. He had broken out about twenty-five acres between two major acequias, but held no rights in either because his fields were considered "new lands."

During the previous few years, the area had enjoyed ample rainfall and farmers with established rights had allowed Rodríguez to irrigate with surplus water. When weather conditions returned to normal, however, there was hardly enough for the "old lands," those cultivated "beyond the time when the memory of man runneth not to the contrary." Most of the sixty farmers above the Trampas road irrigated narrow strips of less than three acres—much smaller than the tract plowed by Rodríguez. If he secured permanent rights for his new plot, his neighbors would suffer. On June 30, Judge Reuben A. Reeves issued a decree that recognized the mayordomo's denial as entirely proper. Since the community owned the acequia system, new users must have consent from a majority of landowners to obtain rights. Use of surplus water in times of plenty failed to create a precedent.[31] In a later case at Taos, however, the court ruled that, when a surplus *was* available, ditch officials must allow water to needy appropriators, even those with junior status, until the stream fell to its normal level.[32]

*Membership and Mayordomos*

Questions surrounding ditch membership continued to plague the courts. In 1899, Jesús H. Sánchez, a landowner from Valencia plaza below Albuquerque sued the mayordomo of La Acequia del Medio for allowing several brothers from the Aragón family to take water claimed by Sánchez. Confusingly, the accused was Sánchez's brother-in-law, Jesús Sánchez y Alarid. According to several witnesses, the community suffered heavy flood damage in 1884 when the Rio Grande rose out of its banks, ripping out large portions of the Medio. After the inundation, ditch owners, planned to repair the breaks, but the Aragóns' father, Manuel Aragón y Baca, refused to participate. Instead, he chose to help build a new canal known as the Acequia de Picurí. In the eyes of many, the Aragón family thus forfeited their rights in the Medio. Unfortunately, the Picurí never served the Aragón lands very well, probably because of faulty engineering. After fifteen years of frustration, don Manuel's sons decided to rejoin the Acequia del Medio, if possible, offering Sánchez y Alarid one hundred ewes as a fee for obtaining permission from the disgruntled parciantes. Eager to earn his commission, the mayordomo managed to line up some support for readmission, but found his own brother-in-law adamantly opposed. To preserve the windfall, Sánchez y Alarid offered to change sides. With a disarming lack of scruples, he proposed to drop the matter entirely if Jesús H. Sánchez and his allies would each give him ten sheep. The suit dragged on for two years, but ended suddenly when the plaintiff died, perhaps allowing the Aragón brothers to regain rights in the Medio, with or without a payoff to the mayordomo.[33]

As administrators of the all-important community acequias, mayordomos held great power, so that elections for the office were hotly contested, sometimes causing disputes that ended in court. At the village of La Mesa, below Las Cruces, for example, Justice of the Peace Albino Gómez, as required by law, scheduled the annual election for ditch officers, naming January 4, 1892. Charles V. Mead and José Sierra opposed Anastacio Villescas and Atanacio Gutiérrez for positions as mayordomo and assistant mayordomo respectively. After the polling, Gómez declared Mead and Sierra as winners, but their opponents claimed the election to be illegal, and, together with their followers, refused to turn out for fatigue work in the ditch three weeks later. On February 6, Mead and Sierra filed suit in district court, requesting Judge John R. McFie to issue an injunction to prevent further interference by the dissidents. Immediately, fifty-four citizens of La Mesa petitioned the court to intervene, claiming that the election had been held illegally and had resulted from a conspiracy between Mead, Sierra, and Justice Gómez.

The defendants reiterated that view in their answer to the suit, and they asserted further that Gómez had failed to appear at the appointed place to oversee the election, which was eventually held at ten o'clock at night in a private residence. They also said that the voting had been conducted on the basis of lands owned, rather than "one man, one vote," as required by the regulation drawn up when the town was founded in 1857. During the hearings, one witness went so far as to state that Gómez engineered the plaintiffs' election in order to obtain water for his own homestead entry just west of the placita. Strong community support for the defendants failed to impress Judge McFie, however, who confirmed the plaintiffs in office, largely on the basis of affidavits from several prominent citizens.[34]

In similar fashion, feeling ran high during the annual elections in 1889 at Valencia, in which Jesús Sánchez y Alarid, who later served as mayordomo of the Acequia del Medio, sought the same office in the Acequia de Picurí. After the votes had been counted, Justice Leandro Abeita declared that Sánchez had defeated his only opponent, Quirino Zamora, and promised to give him a certificate of office. Later, however, the justice refused to surrender the document, causing Sánchez y Alarid to appeal to Judge William H. Brinker for a writ of mandamus. In court, Abeita pointed out that, according to ditch bylaws, only owners or tenants of irrigable lands under the ditch were entitled to vote for officers. As excitement mounted on election day, Sánchez and his partisans had been guilty of "riotous and disorderly conduct," herding large numbers of ineligible voters to the polls, probably with a liberal distribution of aguardiente.

Thus, he claimed victory under false pretenses, a wrong undiscovered until the official canvas had been made. In Abeita's opinion, Zamora had been duly elected, a view in which Judge Brinker concurred.[35]

## Conflicts Between Tradition and Development

As indicated by the previous discussion, district court judges usually rendered equitable decisions in routine cases that involved New Mexico's community acequias, in spite of language differences. When confronted with problems of illegal diversion, apportionment, fatigue duties, elections, or flood damage, court rulings usually conformed to expectations of the Hispano population and were similar to those handed down by previous administrations. However, when conflict arose between traditional institutions and the development projects promoted by Anglo entrepreneurs, the issues proved much more difficult to settle. Sometimes customary procedures for water administration interfered with the desire for profits and economic growth. Disagreements over rights to water had many causes, including the unresolved problem of title to Spanish and Mexican land grants. The struggle for ownership of two overlapping grants on the Rio Gallinas in San Miguel County provides an excellent example.

The difficulty originated in 1819, when Antonio Ortiz, a wealthy sheepman from Santa Fe, received a large grant southeast of present Las Vegas on the western edge of the buffalo plains. For some years, Ortiz grazed his flocks on the grant's lush pastures, but eventually, pressure from hostile Indians forced him to withdraw. Subsequently, twenty-eight families from Nuestra Señora de Guadalupe de la Cuesta (Villanueva) petitioned for farmlands on the Gallinas at Chaperito, unaware that Ortiz previously had claimed much of the same area. On March 10, 1846, New Mexico's Assemblea Departmental approved the Chaperito Grant, a generous tract of irrigable bottomland surrounded by commons for grazing and wood cutting. In customary fashion, the settlers established a new community, building dams and acequias, and plowing fields to be seeded. Except for one or two brief intervals, they managed to maintain continuous possession, undaunted by Indian depredations.

In 1857, after New Mexico had become a U.S. territory, the heirs of Antonio Ortiz presented a claim to their father's grant before William Pelham, surveyor general of New Mexico, the official responsible for reviewing land titles derived from Spain and Mexico. Following an inadequate investigation, Pelham's successor, Alexander P. Wilbar, recommended confirmation by Congress, despite the occupation of several hundred settlers at Chaperito. With congressional approval, the U.S. General Land Office delivered a patent for almost 164,000 acres in 1877 to Stephen B. Elkins and Thomas B. Catron, prominent Santa Fe attorneys and notorious land speculators, who had superseded the Ortiz heirs as claimants. With the patent in hand, Elkins, Catron, and their associates began to assert ownership of all lands within the grant boundaries, including the large irrigated tract at Chaperito to which the settlers had enjoyed undisputed title for thirty years. As a preliminary to a sale or development of grant lands, the absentee claimants posted notices at Chaperito, Los Torres, and several other placitas, ordering the residents to vacate the premises and to refrain from pasturing livestock or cutting timber—on lands the villagers regarded as their own. Until that time, most of them had never heard of the Antonio Ortiz grant.[36]

Although Catron and the others made no serious attempt to evict anyone after posting the handbills, the settlers protested the adverse claim at a public meeting, in which they asserted that the Ortiz grant had been void under Mexican law (presumably through abandonment). Because the population of Chaperito had grown enormously since 1846, rising to 1,500 according to one estimate, the situation threatened many people.

Nevertheless, some years passed before community lenders submitted their own petition for confirmation of the Chaperito grant to Surveyor General George W. Julian.[37] At the same time, grant residents also began a major expansion of their irrigation system, possibly to strengthen their claim of ownership by attracting additional families. In January 1888, laborers started building a large dam across the Gallinas at Los Torres to store irrigation water for one thousand acres of arable land on the river's west bank. They also laid out a double-branched acequia, five miles long, six feet wide, and three feet deep. To accommodate more farmers, they marked off individual lots under the ditch. Greatly alarmed, the owners of the Ortiz grant filed a suit in equity on February 7 in San Miguel County district court, seeking an injunction to block further construction.[38] By then, Elkins had sold his share of the grant, while Catron had increased his interest. New investors included Julius G. Day, a New Haven businessman who later owned the famous Bell Ranch, and Wilson Waddingham, a Canadian-born promoter with large holdings in other land grants. An enthusiastic supporter of irrigation both for general economic growth and personal profit, Waddingham worked tirelessly to further ambitious colonization schemes on the Pablo Montoya and Pedro Armendáriz grants, located east of the Ortiz on the Canadian River and below Socorro along the Rio Grande, respectively.[39] Obviously, the Ortiz grant offered similar opportunities, not to be thwarted by upstart squatters.

Responding to the complaint, Francis Downs, attorney for the Chaperito people, denied that the plaintiffs owned the disputed lands, challenged the validity of the Ortiz grant, and advanced their own title. They also claimed a water right in the Gallinas dating back to the founding of Chaperito in 1846. As requested, the presiding judge then issued an injunction barring further construction, and appointed John H. Koogler of Las Vegas as a special master to take testimony and make a report to the court. After reviewing the evidence,

Koogler recommended in favor of the plaintiffs, largely because their title was based on a patent issued by the federal government. In his report the master argued that, "even if the defendants owned all the water in the river, that fact would not give them the right to take possession of another person's land on which to use it." His reasoning failed to convince the court, however. Relying on a legal distinction, Judge James O'Brien dismissed the suit in equity, finding that the plaintiffs had "a remedy at law" for their grievances, which meant that they could initiate a lawsuit for damages.[40]

Undismayed, Waddingham, Catron, et al. appealed to New Mexico's Supreme Court, where they secured a reversal and a partial victory on February 6, 1892. The high court justices disagreed with their colleague's opinion, ruling that the action in equity should be sustained to prevent a multiplicity of compensation suits for improvements on the lands in question. To resolve the issue, they remanded the case to district court, ordering appointment of a special master to determine the extent of lands possessed by the defendants and the proportion of water from the Gallinas used for irrigation. Appropriation of any additional lands or construction of new irrigation works was forbidden.[41]

After the supreme court decision, the case fell into judicial limbo for sixteen years. Although it was continued on the district court docket, no special master was named and the questions of land ownership and rights to water remained unresolved. In 1899, Wilson Waddingham died suddenly of apoplexy, leaving his affairs in total confusion, which injured Catron financially since their business arrangements were inextricably intertwined. During settlement of the estate, Catron received the deceased's interest in the Ortiz grant in 1905, increasing his share to 75 percent in return for assuming some debts he had incurred jointly with Waddingham. The remaining 25 percent belonged to Day, a reluctant partner. While Catron and Day agreed on little else, they both wanted desperately to sell the grant.

An opportunity seemed to present itself in 1908, when Don A. MounDay, of Topeka, Kansas, signed a contract to buy the Ortiz grant in increments at four dollars per acre. General manager of the American Sugar Manufacturing and Refining Company, MounDay revived the dream of an irrigated empire on the Gallinas by announcing grandiose plans to build a large sugar refinery on the grant, which would be colonized by beet farmers on small plots. A branch railroad down the valley was a necessary part of the scheme. The hustler from Topeka soon mounted an aggressive sales campaign over a wide area to merchandise five-acre parcels, complete with water rights that had not yet been established.[42] To expedite sales and clarify the issue of irrigation rights, Catron revived the suit against the Chaperito settlers, which had been dormant since 1892. On the attorney's petition, a compliant court appointed William E. Gortner, brother of Catron's law partner, as special master.[43] Two years later, Catron hired a professional engineer to map the settlers' claims and locate irrigation ditches at Chaperito. Evidently, Catron intended to use some Chaperito acequias to establish water rights for the beet farmers.[44]

Fortunately for the settlers, the beet sugar promotion scheme soon fell apart. In the fall of 1910, Catron began to receive inquiries from potential investors concerning MounDay's character and financial status. A particularly plaintive letter came from a Midwestern widow, fearful of losing her nest egg, who asked if the sugar company had cleared title to its lands, opened the refinery, or built the railroad.[45] Catron also caught wind of other trouble from H. B. Hening, secretary of the territorial bureau of immigration: gross misrepresentations were being made by the promotor's salesmen. Despite these signals, neither Catron or Hening wanted to jeopardize the economic development promised by MounDay's projects by making untimely accusations. Eventually, the smooth-talking MounDay failed to make the required payments on the Ortiz grant, forcing Catron to take it back. Not long afterwards, federal prosecutors obtained convictions against MounDay and his wife for mail fraud.[46]

Although unresolved by the courts, the uproar on the Gallinas exemplifies some of the cultural conflict resulting from land and water litigation at the end of the nineteenth century. First, the surveyor general's incompetent investigation of title to the Ortiz grant endangered the rights of the settlers at Chaperito. Then the territorial court system bogged down in procedural questions and failed to find a practical solution after four years of expensive litigation. Finally, by upholding the injunction that barred expansion of Chaperito's irrigation system, the justices unfairly prevented the settlers from occupying farmlands to which they were entitled and left them vulnerable to the threat of massive development by outside capitalists.

### The Incorporation Act: Rights-of-Way for Pipelines

On some occasions, Hispanos and Pueblo Indians alike found their water rights endangered by large-scale irrigation projects that blossomed all over the territory following passage of the incorporation act of 1887. That legislation allowed companies to obtain right-of-way for lands or pipelines by condemnation, with no requirement that they themselves be landowners. As a result, water increasingly became a commodity to be bought or sold and used wherever the owner desired. In earlier times, it had been regarded as a necessary prerequisite to subsistence agriculture tied to the land on which it was used.

A corporation formed at the end of 1897 by a group of Albuquerque attorneys and businessmen to cash in on the irrigation bonanza illustrates the point. Although the project that they proposed was many times larger, the bitter dispute over right-of-way closely resembled the conflict between Cristóbal García and his neighbors in 1733. Known as the Albuquerque Land and Irrigation

Company, the company's purpose was to supply water from the Rio Grande for irrigation and colonization on undeveloped lands through a system of reservoirs, canals, ditches, and pipelines. With a huge capacity of 210 cubic feet per second, the main canal would run from just below the pueblo of San Felipe, along the river's east bank to the Santa Fe railroad bridge near the pueblo of Isleta, a distance of thirty-five miles. Early in January 1898, company officials hired an engineer, who began to plot a route for the canal north of Albuquerque. Immediately, the surveyors encountered furious opposition from Hispano farmers and their Pueblo neighbors at Sandía and San Felipe, who forcibly ejected the intruders at gunpoint. Abashed, the company filed two lawsuits in district court requesting injunctions to prevent further interference with the work. The first complaint named Tomás C. Gutiérrez, Pedro Griego y Apodaca, Jesús Zamora, Benito Jaramillo, and León Montoya as defendants; the second was directed against the pueblos of Sandía, San Felipe and Santa Ana. Because of the intense feelings in the Albuquerque area, the cases were moved to Santa Fe County, where they proceeded on a parallel track.[47]

The opposing attorneys opened the proceedings before Judge John R. McFie with statements explaining their respective positions. The plaintiffs emphasized those sections of the 1887 incorporation act that allowed irrigation companies to enter private property and condemn any lands needed for right-of-way. In turn, the defendants countered that the company owned no land under the proposed canal, had no reservoir sites for water storage, had not secured any water rights in the Rio Grande, and had negotiated no contracts with landowners for water distribution. Furthermore, they declared that they and thousands of other irrigators downstream had fully appropriated the river's flow many years before. By building the big canal, the plaintiffs intended to tie up the entire stream and distribute its resources "for pecuniary profit and speculation." Responding to these charges, company attorneys denied that the Rio Grande had been fully appropriated, calling attention to water wasted each year by the community acequias and the large amounts unused during the winter months. Indignantly, they declared that the enterprise had not been organized for speculation, but to develop and conserve water presently dissipated without benefit to anyone. Most important, they disavowed any intention of interfering with vested rights held by some twenty community ditches that originated between San Felipe and Isleta. During arguments concerning existence of surplus water in the Rio Grande, the court heard testimony from Philip E. Harroun, a civil engineer whose survey for the irrigation company had sparked the lawsuits. Depending on measurement techniques pioneered at Embudo by Frederick H. Newell, Harroun explained that the river usually carried some excess, except during the summer months of the driest years, a statement extremely favorable to the plaintiffs.[48]

With the evidence presented, Judge McFie retired to draft a long opinion for the Gutiérrez case that clarified the reasoning behind his forthcoming decision. Carefully crafted, it set forth the attitudes prevailing among the Anglo elite toward irrigation development in New Mexico and the dual system for water management that had evolved there.

Concerning the community acequia, the judge wrote: "I do not underestimate the present ditch system, in some respects it is very good and so long as it is in existence its status and rights must be upheld by the courts; but it is not an economical system." According to McFie, "it would seem strange that a system more than one hundred years old could not be improved." The judge also believed that the territorial legislators had well understood the community acequia, its strengths and weaknesses, as they debated alternatives for change. Although the lawmakers had no desire to destroy the old ways or impair existing rights, they wished to provide "a more modern and improved system for irrigation in the future." Thus, they had passed the incorporation bill to facilitate the agglomeration of capital necessary for large construction.

"Canal companies," McFie wrote, "are deemed beneficial in development of the country and the right of eminent domain is accorded to them to facilitate their operations." The right of condemnation had been granted, however, with two conditions: the land must be taken for a "public purpose," and surplus water must be available. Citing precedents from railroad and highway construction, the judge found that canals clearly served a public purpose. As for the second condition, he relied on data provided by Harroun to rule that a surplus did exist beyond the needs of the twenty community ditches. Since additional usage probably depended on off-season storage, McFie added that the court "could not accept the view that the corporation does not intend to build reservoirs, even though it now lacks the means to do so"—a dictum portending total victory for the irrigation company.[49]

As suggested by his opinion, Judge McFie handed down decrees favorable to the development interests in each of the two cases under consideration. Legally incorporated under New Mexico statutes, the irrigation company was entitled to exercise the right of eminent domain, to build a canal across defendants' lands, and to divert surplus water from the Rio Grande. By preventing construction, the defendants had acted unlawfully, therefore, the plaintiff was entitled to a permanent injunction barring such actions in the future. Defendants' rights as prior appropriators remained undisturbed, but all court costs from the suits were assessed against them. Dissatisfied with the outcome, both Pueblos and Hispanos appealed to the territorial Supreme Court, but, in January 1900, that body reaffirmed McFie's ruling without a single dissent.[50] Thus, the losers faced the inconvenience of an enormous channel dividing their properties and increased competition for irrigation water from the Rio Grande. Of greater significance, the courts, by ruling that irrigation companies could act as an "intermediate agency" and not necessarily as a consumer, served to separate the traditional ties between land and water.

## Community Politics

At times, opposing factions within a community wrestled for control of water resources as part of a larger contest for economic and political domination. A situation of that kind divided Socorro's citizens in the mid-1880s, as recently arrived Anglos challenged the Hispano establishment for supremacy in the town's government. Before the railroad arrived in 1880, Socorro had been merely an undistinguished village nestled on the west bank of the Rio Grande. Suddenly, cheap transportation allowed exploitation of valuable mineral resources in the nearby mountains, bringing unexpected prosperity to the region. The railroad also brought a flood of immigrants from Eastern states and foreign countries that increased Socorro's population from 1,200 to 4,500 within a few years. Unfortunately, the influx caused a soaring crime rate and a breakdown in law enforcement—common problems in Western boom towns. Disgusted by the performance of county officials, some Anglo firebrands organized a vigilance committee whose activities were largely directed against Hispano offenders, which split the citizenry along ethnic lines. Hoping to create a more stable society similar to those they had known before, the newcomers led an effort to incorporate the town, attaining temporary success in January 1882.[51] Thereafter, newly elected Anglo municipal officials began to claim jurisdiction over the Hot Springs Ditch, a community acequia that had supplied water for irrigation and household uses since Socorro's establishment. Originating at a bountiful spring just below the sierra, La Acequia del Ojo Caliente, as it had always been known, was managed by a mayordomo elected annually in the usual way.[52]

An impasse ensued after the town government appointed L. M. Cox as "water master" of the ditch, an action that caused a confrontation with Jacinto Gallegos, the mayordomo voted into office in January 1883. A year later, Justice of the Peace William E. Kelly refused to authorize the next regular election, as required by territorial law. For several months, town police threatened to jail the mayordomo as he vied with Cox for control of the ditch. According to Gallegos, night-riding vigilantes intimidated "Mexican" water users until, suddenly, for unknown reasons, municipal officials withdrew their claim of jurisdiction in June and permitted the election to take place. Peace was restored for the rest of the year, but the issue flared again in the following spring when the town tried to reassert its authority. On February 2, 1885, voters approved a $30,000 bond issue for construction of a modern water works in Socorro, a plan that seems to have depended on the disputed spring as a source of supply.[53] Tensions increased after March 12, when Cox complained formally to Justice Kelly that Gallegos, the reelected mayordomo, had illegally cut and obstructed the

Hot Springs Ditch. As mayordomo, Gallegos audaciously accepted full responsibility and pleaded guilty. Kelly then imposed a fine of fifteen dollars plus
costs, a verdict that caused the mayordomo to appeal to district court and post
a $250 bond.[54] Immediately, leaders of Socorro's Hispano community rallied to
his support, filing a suit of their own in the name of 150 ditch owners against
the city, Mayor F. A. Thompson, City Clerk Samuel C. Meek, and Justice Kelly.
The plaintiffs included Juan José Baca, a wealthy merchant, and Candelario
García, a leading opponent of incorporation who represented Socorro County
in the territorial legislature.

In their complaint, Baca and his associates established ownership of the Ojo
Caliente acequia, reviewed its history, and stated that Jacinto Gallegos served
as the duly elected mayordomo. By illegally taking possession of the ditch, the
defendants prevented Gallegos from performing his duties and caused his arrest. To prevent further interference, they asked the court to issue an injunction
in the customary manner. Responding to these charges, the defendants petitioned for dismissal, claiming both spring and ditch as city property under the
incorporation act and denying that Gallegos still held office. Each side then submitted a sheaf of affidavits to the court in support of their respective positions.
A delay followed in which the opposing attorneys worked out a compromise
that gave the ditch owners at least a temporary victory. Reluctantly, the defendants agreed not to interfere with the Ojo Caliente acequia, or its mayordomo,
"unless or until the city acquires and pays for complainants' rights by condemnation in accordance with the law of the territory."[55]

The settlement ended the battle but not the war. Many of Socorro's Hispano
citizens continued to oppose incorporation as a means of expressing resentment
toward aggressive Anglos, vigilante harassment, the water situation, and a host
of other issues. Led by Candelario García, Socorro's legislative delegation in
Santa Fe pushed bills to disincorporate the town—an action that would have
endangered the bond issue and prevented condemnation of rights in the Hot
Springs Ditch. Although the controversy remained unresolved in 1889, ethnic
tensions eventually subsided and municipal government managed to continue.[56]

Certainly the longest and most acrimonious fight for control of community
water occurred at Tularosa, a small placita in south-central New Mexico on the
west slope of the Sacramento Mountains. Ironically, in view of the subsequent
struggle, Tularosa's founders migrated from villages on the Rio Grande to es-
cape the recurrent floods that sometimes devastated parts of the river valley. In
1862, defying the threat from hostile Mescalero Apaches who occupied the Sacramentos, about sixty Hispanos from Doña Ana, La Mesilla, and Las Cruces settled at the mouth of Tularosa Canyon. Ten families of Tiwa-speaking Pueblo
Indians from Isleta del Sur migrated with them. Almost immediately, the newcomers constructed the obligatory community acequia to accommodate crops

and household needs. At first, the settlers lived in a collection of huts (*chozas*) built within a long trench dug for defense. After a few years, however, they laid out a townsite on a grid plan, each citizen receiving a building site (*solar*) and a garden plot (*hortaliza*). Landholders also obtained a right to twelve hours of water from the ditch, more than necessary to irrigate the small parcels cultivated at that time. As years passed, the settlers increased the water supply by extending the ditch and draining *tulares* (swampy places) up the canyon, which allowed larger areas to be farmed. Prodded by Major Lawrence G. Murphy, who managed a far-flung mercantile empire from Lincoln, across the Sacramentos, community leaders petitioned U.S. officials for a patent to their lands. This was granted in 1875.[57]

During the same year, Anglo outsiders challenged the villagers' rights to water from the Rio Tularosa. In 1871, several former soldiers took up homesteads in the canyon above Tularosa and broke out fields for planting. Attracted to the area while serving at Fort Stanton, across the mountains, most of the veterans had come to the territory with the California Column, a volunteer unit mustered to support Union forces in New Mexico during the Civil War. Serious trouble erupted after Andrew Wilson, John Walters, James West, and Wesley Fields built dams across the river for irrigation. When angry Hispano farmers ripped out the diversions, an armed confrontation ensued that continued until troops from Fort Stanton arrived to impose an uneasy truce. In February 1877, the two factions signed an agreement granting the village a right-of-way through the canyon to the river's headwaters for an extension of their acequia. In return, the canyon people received a water right for lands then in production and for other tracts to be cultivated thereafter, a proviso that guaranteed further conflict, since every homesteader expanded his irrigated acreage as fast as possible. Each spring, hostilities flared anew, culminating on April 18, 1881, in a gun battle five miles above Tularosa in which Cruz Padilla, a Doña Ana County deputy sheriff, and three other Hispanos died while trying to arrest Anglos taking water illegally.[58] Once again, the army restored order, but failed to bring a permanent solution. Although the feuding continued unabated, the focus shifted from ditch banks along the Tularosa to courtrooms in various county seats.

On June 24, 1885, several settlers from Tularosa filed suit in Doña Ana County district court charging that Wilson, Walters, Fields, and other canyon residents had taken water illegally, causing great damage to crops and fruit trees in the town. As their legal representative, the townspeople chose William L. Rynerson, a Las Cruces attorney and former legislator who had previously served with the California Column. Rynerson proved to be an unfortunate selection, however, because of an irreconcilable conflict of interest. For some years, the attorney and his partners, John H. Riley and Pantaleón Sandoval, had been acquiring parcels of land in the Tularosa Canyon, which they planned to use as headquarters for a large cattle operation on the surrounding public domain. Testimony before Special Master L. W. Lenoir revealed that much of the unlawful diversion had occurred on lands recently purchased by the partnership, a disclosure that caused Rynerson to withdraw from the case in embarrassment. The townspeople replaced him with other lawyers, but they were unable to present convincing witnesses before the special master, who issued a report favoring the defendants. Judge John R. McFie dismissed the suit on December 5, 1889, leaving the question of water rights on the Rio Tularosa unresolved.[59] More important, the arrival in the region of outside capitalists with powerful political connections complicated the problem enormously.

## The Complications of Capitalism

### A Continuation of the Tularosa Story

As noted previously, the advent of rail transportation stimulated tremendous growth in New Mexico's livestock industry. To cash in on the so-called beef bonanza, investors organized financial combines such as the partnership formed in 1885 between Riley, Rynerson, and Sandoval. Later, Sandoval sold out to his partners and the ubiquitous Thomas B. Catron, the territory's leading Republican politician. On March 28, 1890, Riley, Rynerson, Catron, and two associates incorporated the enterprise as the Tularosa Land and Cattle Company, issuing 2,500 shares of stock valued at $100 each. From the outset, the shareholders contemplated a much wider range of activities than ranching, as indicated by the articles of incorporation. Article V stated an intention "to purchase, lease, buy and sell water and water rights and charge rental and toll therefor." Under Article VI, the firm proposed "to appropriate, convey and use the waters of the said Rio Tularosa" for irrigation, domestic, and livestock purposes, and "to construct the necessary canals and ditches in connection therewith."[60] Managed by aggressive capitalists with important political connections, the cattle company replaced the Anglo homesteaders as the villagers' principal opponent in the war for water from the Rio Tularosa.

The fight began anew on April 28, 1893, after Cesario Durán, Tularosa's constable, arrested a company employee on a complaint from Mayordomo Severiano Gallegos for taking water without authorization. Brought before Justice of the Peace Henry K. Parker, the miscreant was fined five dollars and costs for his misdeed. Determined to prevent establishment of a precedent, the cattle company filed suit in district court against Parker, Gallegos, Durán, Doña Ana County Sheriff Rosalio Baldonado, and all five commissioners of the town ditch, asking for an injunction to stop further interference. With Judge Albert B. Fall presiding, company attorneys reviewed the high points of the perennial struggle and based their case on the 1877 agreement allowing irrigation in the canyon. In rebuttal, the defendants denied validity of the contract, asserting that it had been written in English, a language unfamiliar to town representatives. Attempting once again to impose a settlement, Judge Fall set forth a five-point order on December 15, 1894. Under its terms, the cattle company received permission to irrigate lands then cultivated, but was barred from future expansion. Each day, from 8:00 A.M. to 6:00 P.M., the company was allowed exclusive use of the river's flow, with the stipulation that a single "head" of water, three feet wide and two inches deep, must run at all times for domestic use in the town. To increase the stream's flow, Tularosa townspeople were authorized to drain ciénegas and tule lands in the canyon. Any diversion by the cattle company into storage reservoirs could take place only in November, December, and January. Finally, all costs of the lawsuit must be assumed by the plaintiffs.[61]

Undoubtedly, the town of Tularosa suffered a severe setback from Judge Fall's decision, which, for the first time, divided the river under a time schedule without regard for priorities. Further reversals were yet to come. During the next decade, competition for irrigation water increased throughout the valley, as population continued to grow. At the headwaters, agents for the Mescalero Apaches encouraged irrigated farming on the reservation to make the tribe more self-sufficient. Meanwhile, Anglo immigrants to Tularosa plowed up more desert lands near the village that were planted to a variety of crops. Real estate prices rose on rumors that a railroad would soon be built from El Paso through the valley to tap the gold mines at White Oaks and the coal deposits near Capitan. Although drainage projects among the tulares in the canyon provided more water, the cultivated acreage below increased at a faster pace.

As demand for water grew, Tularosa's first Hispano settlers began to separate their water rights from the hortalizas granted to them in 1862. Some began using water pertaining to the hortalizas on fields beyond the town boundaries; some sold their water rights to others who also irrigated outside the original townsite. Because of poor record keeping, landholders in town occasionally continued to receive water from the mayordomo after all rights had been conveyed away. Gradual alienation of rights in the town jeopardized Hispano control of the acequia system. Attempting to bring order out of chaos, community leaders incorporated the acequia under the legislative act of 1887 as the Tularosa Reservoir and Irrigation Company. This was on December 7, 1894—a few days before Judge Fall handed down his decision.[62] Subsequently, acequia officers attempted to identify those persons entitled to receive water based on their participation in annual labor for ditch maintenance. After an investigation, they compiled a list of 107 members that was duly recorded with the clerk of Doña Ana County in Las Cruces.

As they contemplated changing conditions in the region, owners of the

Tularosa Land and Cattle Company discerned possibilities for profit from a speculation in water rights. To achieve that goal, they made overtures to the new managers of the acequia system who proved to be most cooperative. In 1904, the Tularosa Reservoir and Irrigation Company reorganized as the Tularosa Community Ditch. The officers distributed printed by-laws to the 107 members, henceforth to be known as "shareholders." Significantly, the by-laws included provisions to levy assessments for legal expenses when necessary "to protect and preserve the waters of said ditch."

Litigation was not long in coming. On November 29, 1904, Judge Fall, who had returned to private practice and served as counsel to the ditch company, filed a suit in Otero County district court against the Tularosa Land and Cattle Company. In a letter to Catron, John Riley explained the matter as follows:

> The understanding between Judge Fall and myself was to this effect. That the Indians were using a large amount of water that they were not entitled to and that he would bring a suit for the water users at Tularosa against the Indians and all others up the canon (including ourselves in a friendly way) and that you would aid him draw up the papers. That while the suit was pending we would endeavor to purchase water rights and consolidate them and fight the Indians for the water they were using and we would arrange an amicable arrangement by which Judge Fall you and I would make some money out of it.[63]

Riley's representation to the contrary, the suit involved much more than some excessive diversion by the Mescaleros. Unfortunately, the case file containing documents from the suit is missing, but the court's final decree has been reprinted.

After more than four years of litigation, Judge Edward A. Mann rendered a modified final decree on April 29, 1909 intended to reapportion the Rio Tularosa among the several contending parties. Declaring offhandedly that the river ordinarily carried enough water for those entitled to it, the judge began by ruling that the Tularosa Community Ditch need only furnish water to solares in the town once every two weeks. Furthermore, hortalizas that no longer had water rights could not be irrigated at all except during the winter up to March 1, a heavy restriction on landholders in the town. Although the Mescaleros and others on the reservation had been wrongfully taking too much water, Mann decided that they had acquired a prescriptive right to irrigate approximately 470 acres near the headwaters.

Finally, by prior appropriation, the Tularosa Community Ditch was entitled to the river's entire flow, but, under the stipulation of 1894, the Tularosa Land and Cattle Company retained daily use of the stream from 8:00 AM to 6:00 PM. A number of other settlers in the canyon had also secured prescriptive rights for 246 acres. To implement distribution, Mann set up a time schedule similar to the one imposed earlier by Judge Fall.[64] A year after Mann's decree had been issued, Catron and Riley completed their financial coup by deeding all cattle company lands in the canyon to the Tularosa Community Ditch people in return for fifty water rights in the acequia system. According to George Curry, New Mexico's governor from 1907 to 1910, who represented the ditch company during the negotiations, the rights were valued at one thousand dollars each.[65]

As a result of legal maneuvering by the cattle company and officers of the community ditch, the townspeople found themselves shut out from management of the acequia system originally built for their benefit. Although they had not been included in the recent adjudication, Judge Mann's decree left them at the mercy of those listed as water rights holders. Attempting to fight back and regain control of the precious water supply, a large number of village residents formed a new organization in 1909. Known as the "Community Ditches or Acequias of Tularosa Townsite," the membership proceeded to conduct regular elections for commissioners and a mayordomo. Leadership of the resistance movement included Ralph S. Connell, a recent arrival from Omaha who was the son of W. J. Connell, a prominent attorney and former Nebraska congressman. With his father as absentee partner, Ralph Connell had established an experimental farm just east of Tularosa, where he raised poultry on a large scale and planted exotic crops, such as Bermuda onions and cut flowers. Hoping for a peaceful settlement of the ditch war, officers of the new organization met with their counterparts from the community ditch and naively asked them to surrender control. What they received in return was "a horse laugh," as Connell recalled later.

Seeking relief elsewhere, the Community Ditches or Acequias of Tularosa then filed suit on April 1, 1910 in Otero County district court, challenging the legal status of the Tularosa Community Ditch and requesting an injunction to prevent the latter from interfering in acequia management. After lengthy hearings, Judge Edward R. Wright decided that the plaintiffs' action was not a suitable means to determine rights of the opposing parties and dismissed the suit without prejudice on July 11, 1911. Still determined, the plaintiffs appealed to the territorial Supreme Court, which, on December 23, upheld Judge Wright. In their opinion, the justices suggested that the plaintiffs file a suit *quo warranto*, the proper action to oust a corporate entity exercising powers not conferred by law.[66]

Connell and his followers then began a new lawsuit, quo warranto, in Otero County district court to determine which of the two corporations was legally empowered to control the ditch. During the trial, W. J. Connell came out from Omaha to join Frank Clancy, New Mexico's attorney general, as representatives for the plaintiffs, while the wily Thomas B. Catron took charge of the defense. The elder Connell opened the proceedings by claiming that the Tularosa Community Ditch had been organized illegally, that it represented the so-called shareholders rather than the community, and that the town's founders had been defrauded by the apportionment made after the 1904 lawsuit in which they had not participated. In response, Catron asserted that his clients were the legal successors of the first settlers who, through the years, had simply conveyed whatever rights they had to others. Once again, the testimony was voluminous and the hearings dragged on for many months as tension mounted in the community, completely polarized by the water issue. At last, on January 11, 1913, Judge Edward L. Medler submitted a decision that favored the plaintiffs, the Community Ditches or Acequias of Tularosa. According to Medler, the water rights claimed by the Tularosa Community Ditch had no basis in law and were void. Owners of land irrigated by the ditch also owned the ditch itself and were entitled to manage and use it by having participated in its construction. Finally, and most important, under New Mexico law, the separation of water rights from land for sale or barter had no application to public acequias or community ditches.[67]

Catron immediately appealed Medler's decision to the Supreme Court, but, before the justices could render a verdict, tragedy struck Tularosa. On June 17, 1914, Ralph S. Connell was ambushed and killed by gunfire east of town as he drove cattle toward the Mescalero agency accompanied by his little daughter and three cowboys. Otero County authorities arrested a belligerent partisan in the water dispute, who had a grudge against Connell, and charged him with murder. When the case came to trial, however, a jury found him "not guilty" because there were no eyewitnesses to the crime.[68]

With emotions running high, the Supreme Court shocked the community again by reversing Judge Medler and sending the quo warranto case back to district court with an order for dismissal. In a long opinion written by Chief Justice Clarence J. Roberts, the Court decided that the Community Ditches or Acequias of Tularosa Townsite was not a legal corporation entitled to administer affairs of the ditch because its officers had been elected unlawfully. Instead of apportioning water according to the amount of land irrigated, every property owner was considered equal in the balloting. Also, elections had been limited to residents of the townsite even though other outside landowners had acquired rights in the ditch. These defects made the organization a legal nonentity. On the other hand, by bringing suit against the Tularosa Community Ditch instead of its individual officers, the plaintiffs had recognized the legal existence of the opposing corporation.

To bring final resolution to the issue, the justices recommended another lawsuit to adjudicate the water rights of each landowner.[69] But after Ralph Connell's death, the townspeople seemed to lack both determination and finances for further litigation. Despite sixty years of strife, the people of Tularosa had lost control of their acequia system. Although the original Hispano settlers had been guilty of poor management during the town's first years, their opponents' aggressive business practices, reinforced by an incomprehensible justice system, eventually did them in.

*Tighter Laws . . . and More Trouble for Hispanos*

During the 1890s, as irrigation expanded throughout the territory, governmental officials recognized a need for a comprehensive code of water law and a centralized agency for its administration. Few changes had been made since the legislature passed the bill in 1887 allowing incorporation of irrigation companies. Tighter regulation came four years later through a statute that required claimants to record future appropriations with county officials, indicating point of diversion, ditch route, volume of water to be used, and construction date. In 1905, lawmakers enacted new water laws and established a new department, the office of the territorial irrigation engineer, to supervise water administration. The engineer was to receive the princely salary of two thousand dollars annually.

Two years later, in 1907, the legislature passed a stronger bill that gave the administrator greater powers and changed his title to that of territorial engineer. In addition to general supervision of the territory's waters, he received authority to make hydrographic surveys to determine water availability, regulate apportionment within various stream systems, and issue permits for new projects.[70] Petitions of that kind were particularly difficult since applicants invariably exaggerated total stream flow and the data necessary for a fair evaluation were often nonexistent.

Although the legislation undoubtedly strengthened water administration in the territory, the new arrangement of 1907, like the court system, caused serious problems for Hispanos accustomed to traditional ways. Eager to promote economic growth, lawmakers failed to provide adequate safeguards for the needs of long-established communities. While officials dutifully gave lip service to existing rights as they processed applications for unappropriated water, their procedures left large loopholes that were easily exploited by sharp operators. The troubles experienced by Nuevo Mexicanos in protecting their rights are exemplified in the disputes between water users in the Taos Valley and Arthur R. Manby, an unprincipled British speculator, who came to the territory in 1883.[71]

During the late 1890s, Manby accumulated a substantial interest in the Antonio Martínez grant, 60,000 acres of valuable land north of Taos recently confirmed by the Court of Private Land Claims. Using native New Mexicans as agents, he had gradually increased his equity by making small purchases from Hispano families who had lived on the grant for generations. By 1902, he had acquired sufficient acreage to bring a lawsuit in district court to quiet title to the grant, a preliminary to its partition.[72] Eventually, he hoped to turn the Martínez lands into a great agricultural empire of irrigated farms and orchards to be manipulated for his own benefit. In 1907, Taos Valley Land Company, a corporation formed by Manby and Eastern investors to exploit the grant, filed applications with Territorial Engineer Vernon J. Sullivan to appropriate water from the Rio Hondo, Rio Lucero, and Arroyo Seco to irrigate 20,000 acres.[73] These streams already failed to satisfy established rights vested in community acequias during dry years, but Hispano parciantes probably remained completely unaware of the company's petition and the dangers presented by it. For his part, Manby hoped to reach agreements with water users along the streams to enlarge and extend their ancient ditch systems as a way to control his construction costs.

Because a recent treaty between the United States and Mexico had guaranteed water from Elephant Butte Dam for farmers on both sides of the border, Manby feared that his plan to divert large amounts from the upper tributaries of the Rio Grande would be opposed by governmental agencies. However, his Santa Fe attorney, Robert C. Gortner, assured him that Sullivan had reacted favorably to preliminary inquiries. Gortner believed that a modest proposal, skillfully presented by an engineer and emphasizing maximum return to the river, would win approval as an economic benefit to the territory. His tactics proved persuasive: in April 1908, the territorial engineer denied the Lucero diversion but approved those for the Hondo and Arroyo Seco.[74] Having cleared the territorial hurdle, Manby turned his attention to Washington D.C., lobbying forcefully among bureaucrats and legislators. In a letter to C. J. Blanchard, a functionary with the U.S. Reclamation Service, he sharply criticized the recent agreement with Mexico, suggesting darkly that the United States representative, Colonel Anson Mills, had schemed to assure water for a large irrigation project of his own near El Paso. How much better it would be, Manby continued, to develop an area of superior land in the upper tributaries, such as that owned by the Taos Valley Land Company, in which several retired naval officers and other influential Eastern families had invested substantially! Such initiatives must not be thwarted by government; to the contrary, they

> should receive every assistance, more particularly as this is a section that has been regarded as a seat of revolution and antagonistic to American progress and settlement; the colonization of these lands by good American farmers will do more than anything else to carry out the policy of the President, and develop this country and pave the way to statehood.[75]

Blanchard's reaction to Manby's flag-waving is not extant, but a lack of funds prevented the Englishman from implementing his most ambitious irrigation schemes and eventually bankruptcy terminated his dreams of empire.

But even as he failed, the arrogant Englishman knew how to manipulate the system, pressuring bureaucrats and elected officials for his own advantage. The administration process that evolved at the turn of the century favored speculators such as Manby over descendants of the original Hispano settlers who had been irrigating their lands for centuries. Unfamiliar with engineering concepts and technical jargon always presented in a foreign tongue, New Mexicans found themselves at a disadvantage during court sessions or administrative hearings that determined their rights. More important, decision making shifted from locally elected officials to bureaucrats in Santa Fe who were unfamiliar with conditions and customs at the grassroots. As a result, residents of remote villages found it difficult or impossible to participate in proceedings of vital importance.

During the thirty years preceding statehood, procedures for water administration underwent profound changes in New Mexico. Rail transportation brought a huge population influx and linked the territory to the national economy for the first time. Seeking opportunities for profit, newly arrived entrepreneurs initiated large-scale irrigation projects dependent on modern technology and massive capital investments. Increasingly, the new developments conflicted with traditional institutions for water management. Local control slipped away, as county probate courts declined in importance, causing aggrieved water users to seek relief in district courts, a venue dominated by professional attorneys trained in the complexities of English common law. Frequently, district court judges rendered verdicts depending on legal technicalities that failed to resolve the practical issues in question, thus leading to more litigation. Although routine matters were usually adjudicated satisfactorily, cases that ranged traditional users against developers proved much more difficult to settle.

Recognizing that legislation intended for community acequias was inappropriate for enormous water projects, lawmakers attempted to revamp administrative procedures so as to encourage economic growth without disturbing time-honored customs. However, they were not always successful and at the beginning of the new century Hispano irrigators faced growing difficulties as they struggled to control their historic water resources.

# Conclusion

In NEW MEXICO, from the beginning of Spanish settlement to the present, no issue has caused greater concern and controversy than the administration of water. As Coronado and his followers explored the region, they avidly sought reliable water sources to ensure survival; pioneer settlers often established acequias for irrigation before they built houses. Within days of his arrival at San Juan, Oñate had persuaded a large force of Pueblo Indians to scrape out a ditch for his chimerical capital city. A century later, Vargas founded a new villa beside the Rio Santa Cruz, knowing that the residents would find the stream well suited to irrigating their crops.

As settlement spread to new locations during the eighteenth century, governors continued to exhibit similar concern for water supplies before authorizing grants of land. In nascent villages throughout the province, every citizen shared responsibility for building and maintaining the community acequia, which became universally accepted as the customary institution for water administration. Inevitably, population growth increased competition for irrigation water among contending groups. On some streams, parciantes developed a priority system in which newcomers secured rights to any surplus remaining after earlier appropriators had satisfied their needs. As circumstances changed, such arrangements were adjusted accordingly. At a few locations, such as Las Truchas and Desmontes, New Mexicans demonstrated amazing engineering skills to obtain a water supply, constructing sophisticated irrigation works that are still in use today.

Under colonial administration, New Mexico's governors exercised final authority in resolving water issues. Appointed by the king, governors were empowered to name a number of alcaldes mayores as their legal representatives in local jurisdictions. Usually, water litigation originated in the alcaldes' courts; difficult cases went to the governor on appeal, but the latter relied on local officials to conduct investigations. In many instances, authorities appointed a committee of unbiased experts to make an inspection and suggest a solution. Common complaints included illicit appropriation, inequitable apportionment, unfair maintenance assignments, disputed right-of-way, and flood damage. When original water sources on land grants proved inadequate, settlers applied to the official hierarchy for supplementary allocations. Although neighbors occasionally came to blows over illegal preemption, the judicial system kept violence in check and disposed of water cases without difficulty. Unencumbered by legal training, authorities on the frontier depended more on popular values than arcane legalities in rendering decisions. Above all, they endeavored to preserve harmony within the community and avoid factional strife.

Following Mexico's independence from Spain in 1821, New Mexicans attained a greater role in local government through reestablishment of municipal councils. Known as ayuntamientos, the councils had originated in medieval Spain and were revived by the liberal constitution of 1812. Once organized, they relieved provincial governors of responsibility for water management. Popularly elected, council members clearly understood the interests of their constituents and responded readily to public opinion. Although the governmental structure was new, the water issues to be considered remained much the same.

Because of their intimate knowledge of local issues, the ayuntamientos functioned well as government agencies until Mexico's conservative political faction seized national power in 1836. The new regime imposed a centralist constitution that organized the nation into departments and suppressed the ayuntamientos except for the one in Santa Fe. As a department, New Mexico was divided into two prefectures, the Rio Arriba and the Rio Abajo, each administered by a prefect responsible to the governor. The constitution also created new officials—justices of the peace—who functioned much like alcaldes and assumed responsibility for water litigation in their jurisdiction. Their decisions were sometimes appealed to higher authorities, but prefects and governors usually insisted on resolution of water cases in local courts. Although ayuntamiento oversight was more democratic, the centralist regime functioned reasonably well during the period of Mexican rule in New Mexico.

Important changes took place, however, after the United States conquest of New Mexico in 1846. The troops who marched into Santa Fe's plaza on August 18 brought not only a change of sovereignty but also a new form of government. Once New Mexico became a U.S. territory, Hispanos succeeded in reconciling traditional water management with the institutions imposed by the new regime for some years. By gaining control of the territorial legislature and local courts, they preserved time-honored procedures and a high level of community participation. Nevertheless, preservation of local customs became more difficult after 1880, as a technological transformation swept over the territory, placing parciantes in remote villages at an increasing disadvantage.

The coming of the railroad in 1878 suddenly integrated New Mexico into the national economy and brought a new surge in population growth. At the same time, politicians in Washington and in state and territorial capitals recognized the tremendous potential for economic advancement throughout the West offered by large-scale irrigation projects. Entrepreneurs appeared in many locations, looking for profits from irrigated lands and demanding a share of the territory's waters. To assure New Mexico's share of the boom, legislators established new institutions facilitating the capital formation needed for large irrigation projects. As competition for water intensified between developers and traditional users, territorial district courts increasingly assumed jurisdiction in lawsuits to determine the rights of opposing parties. Unfamiliar with English common law, Hispano litigants were hurt by the shift away from local tribunals.

Believing that New Mexico needed a centralized authority for water administration, in 1907 members of the legislature enacted a new code of water law to be implemented by an official, the territorial engineer. Entrusted with great power, the engineer had authority to allocate water in various streams and approve applications for new irrigation projects. With a few minor alterations made since its passage, the 1907 code remains the foundation of water law in New Mexico today.

Although the original bill required recognition of existing water rights, aggressive developers often found ways to circumvent the legislators' intent. Handicapped by a language barrier and lack of technical expertise, Hispanos experienced great difficulties in protecting their traditional institutions after 1907, as decision making gravitated toward bureaucrats in Santa Fe. Recently, as water users have become better informed about governmental procedures, they have formed regional acequia associations for mutual protection, especially during lawsuits to adjudicate priorities. Local participation in water litigation has increased, but ensuring a voice for small communities during the process remains a problem.

# Notes

## Chapter 1

1. George P. Hammond and Agapito Rey, *Don Juan de Oñate, Colonizer of New Mexico, 1595–1628*, 2 vols. (Albuquerque, 1953), 1: 320–23, 346.

2. Juan de Torquemada, *Monarquía Indiana*, 3 vols., Quinta Edición, (Mexico, 1975), 1: 678.

3. François Chevalier, *Land and Society in Colonial Mexico: The Great Hacienda* (Berkeley, 1970): 51; Michael E. Murphy, *Irrigation in the Bajío Region of Colonial Mexico* (Boulder and London, 1986): 124–28.

4. Hammond and Rey, *Don Juan de Oñate*, 1: 484, 2: 626, 634.

5. Ibid., 2: 626, 634, 653, 656, 674, 714–15, 722.

6. Ibid., 2: 1088.

7. Charles Wilson Hackett, ed., *Revolt of the Pueblo Indians of New Mexico and Otermin's Attempted Reconquest, 1680–1682*, trans. Charmion Clair Shelby, 2 vols. (Albuquerque, 1942), 1: 13, 98.

8. Ibid., 1: 101–04.

9. J. Manuel Espinosa, *First Expedition of Vargas into New Mexico, 1692* (Albuquerque, 1940): 86.

10. Spanish Archives of New Mexico (SANM) I, no. 422, Juan Lucero de Godoy, petition for lands, El Paso, January 15, 1693, State Records Center and Archives (SRCA), Santa Fe, N.M.

11. SANM I, no. 476, Roque Madrid, petition for lands, El Paso, September 18, 1693.

12. SANM I, no. 477, Domingo Martín, petition for lands, Santa Fe, March 22, 1695; no. 478, Luis Maese, petition for lands, Santa Fe, March 21, 1695.

13. SANM I, no. 77, Ana Luján, sale of house and land, Santa Fe, September 12, 1701; no. 411, Isabel Jorge, petition for lands, Santa Fe, March 20, 1699; no. 477; no. 478. A measure of volume (1.6 to 2.5 bushels depending on time and place), a fanega also quantified area, i.e., the amount of land needed to sow one fanega of seed. In New Spain, a fanega of corn comprised 8.8 acres, a fanega of wheat 1.5 acres. See Charles Gibson, *The Aztecs Under Spanish Rule: A History of the Indians of the Valley of Mexico, 1519–1810* (Stanford, 1964): 308, 323.

14. J. Manuel Espinosa, *Crusaders of the Río Grande: The Story of Don Diego de Vargas and the Reconquest and Refounding of New Mexico* (Chicago, 1942): 129.

15. Ibid.: 118, 124–28, 188.

16. Ibid.: 187, 227.

17. Ibid.: 221, 225.

18. Myra Ellen Jenkins, "Settlement of the Jurisdiction of La Cañada," in Myra Ellen Jenkins and John O. Baxter, "Settlement and Irrigation in the Santa Cruz-Quemado Watershed," State Engineer Office (Santa Fe, 1986): 1, 5–7, 14–16.

19. SANM I, no. 882, Proceedings in the Settlement of Santa Cruz de la Cañada, 1695, ff. 18–19.

20. Ibid.: f. 27.

21. SANM I, no. 817, Settlement of additional families at Santa Cruz de la Cañada, May 8, 1696.

22. SANM I, no. 741, Francisco Xavier Romero, petition for lands, Santa Cruz de la Cañada, October 17, 1716.

23. SANM I, no. 818, Petition by settlers at Santa Cruz de la Cañada to relocate to Alameda, November 26, 1696.

24. For a detailed study of Vargas's imprisonment and eventual exoneration, see Espinosa, *Crusaders of the Río Grande:* 307–40.

25. A report of the Vargas redistribution of February 13, 1704 is found in Records of the Court of Private Land Claims, no. 194, Santa Cruz de la Cañada Grant, SRCA.

26. Espinosa, *Crusaders of the Río Grande:* 244–47; Charles W. Hackett, ed. *Historical Documents relating to New Mexico, Nueva Vizcaya, and Approaches Thereto, to 1773,* 3 vols. (Washington, 1923–1937), 3: 380.

27. John O. Baxter, *Spanish Irrigation in the Pojoaque and Tesuque Valleys during the Eighteenth and Early Nineteenth Centuries,* State Engineer Office (Santa Fe, 1984): 9–10. See also Fray Angelico Chavez, *Origins of New Mexico Families in the Spanish Colonial Period* (Santa Fe, 1975): 273.

28. SANM I, no. 745, Ignacio Roybal v. Juan de Mestas, Jacona, January 16, 1723.

29. Santa Fe County Deed Records, Book G-1: 20–21, Office of the County Clerk, Santa Fe County Courthouse, Santa Fe, N.M.

30. Records of the Surveyor General (SG) no. 49, Bernabé Montaño Grant, ff. 1–2, SRCA.

31. Ibid.: ff. 2–3.

32. Frank D. Reeve, "The Navaho-Spanish Peace: 1720s–1770s," *New Mexico Historical Review* 34 (January 1959): 38–39.

33. SG no. 27, Town of Las Trampas Grant. The expression *tierras de labor de pan llevar* is usually translated as "lands for wheat growing." Some historians have reasoned that since wheat was usually irrigated in New Spain, the phrase also indicates "irrigated land." See Michael C. Meyer, *Water in the Hispanic Southwest* (Tucson, 1984): 128. For additional discussion, see also Murphy, *Irrigation in the Bajío Region:* 127, n. 43.

34. SANM I, no. 771, Juan de Díos Romero and others, petition for land grant known as Nuestra Señora del Rosario, San Fernando y Santiago del Río de las Truchas, March 5, 1754.

35. See generally, Alfred Barnaby Thomas, *After Coronado: Spanish Exploration Northeast of New Mexico, 1696–1727* (Norman, 1935). For Velez's reaction, see Elizabeth A. H. John, *Storms Brewed in Other Men's Worlds: The Confrontation of Indians, Spanish, and French in the Southwest, 1540–1795* (College Station, 1975): 319–36.

36. Eleanor B. Adams and Fray Angelico Chavez, *The Missions of New Mexico, 1776: A Description by Fray Francisco Atanasio Domínguez with other Contemporary Documents* (Albuquerque, 1951): 217, n. 1; Oakah L. Jones Jr., *Los Paisanos: Spanish Settlers on the Northern Frontier of New Spain* (Norman, 1979): 127–28.

37. SG no. 119, San Miguel del Vado Grant; SG no. 46, Cebolleta Grant; Myra Ellen Jenkins and Spencer Wilson, "Socorro—Facts Not Fancy," *La Crónica de Nuevo Mexico* 20 (March 1985): 3; SG no. 58, Rio Grande del Rancho Grant; SG no. 125, Don Fernando de Taos Grant.

38. SG no. 58, Rio Grande del Rancho Grant; SANM II, no. 1714, Chacón to Salcedo, March 28, 1804. For a summary of Navajo-Hispano relations during this period, See Frank McNitt, *Navajo Wars: Military Campaigns, Slave Raids, and Reprisals* (Albuquerque, 1972): 26–51. Chacón may have underestimated Cebolleta's resources. According to the United States Census conducted in 1850 for Valencia County, Cebolleta then supported 451 persons in ninety-three households and a garrison of 152 U.S. dragoons.

39. SG no. 158, Cristóbal de la Serna Grant; Thomas, *After Coronado:* 38, 165. Although the names are identical, the river indicated here must not be confused with the Rio Trampas, north of Las Truchas.

40. SANM I, no. 759.

41. SANM II, not numbered, Census of Taos jurisdiction, 1790, microfilm copy, roll 23: 259–60.

42. SG no. 58, Rio Grande del Rancho Grant.

43. SG no. 125, Don Fernando de Taos Grant.

44. Ibid.

45. SANM I, no. 1297. This archive includes several documents concerning land titles and settlement at Arroyo Seco that were produced as evidence in an 1826 lawsuit. For a more detailed study of land and water issues in this area, see John O. Baxter, *Spanish Irrigation in Taos Valley,* State Engineer Office (Santa Fe, 1990): 56–73.

46. SANM I, no. 1297; see also, "Statement of Nicolas Sandoval," SG no. 58, Rio Grande del Rancho Grant.

47. Baxter, *Spanish Irrigation in Taos Valley:* 35–37, 59–60.

## Chapter 2

1. Charles R. Cutter, "Judicial Practice in New Spain, 1700–1810," Ph.D., diss., University of New Mexico, 1989: 79, 86–87, 90–91, 114–17.

2. Michael C. Meyer, *Water in the Hispanic Southwest: A Social and Legal History, 1550–1850* (Tucson, 1984): 131; Robert C. West, *The Mining Community in Northern New Spain: The Parral Mining District* (University of California Publications, Ibero-Americana 30, Berkeley and Los Angeles, 1949): 60.

3. Records of the Surveyor General of New Mexico (SG), no. 125, Don Fernando de Taos Grant, State Records Center and Archives, (SRCA) Santa Fe, N.M.

4. Spanish Archives of New Mexico (SANM) I, no. 169, Diego Arias de Quiros, proceedings regarding construction of a pond for irrigation, Santa Fe, 1715–1716, SRCA.

5. For a summary of the quarrel between the two governors, see Ted J. Warner, "Don Félix Martínez and the Santa Fe Presidio, 1693–1730," *New Mexico Historical Review* 45 (October 1970): 269–310.

6. SANM I, no. 169. In his important book, *Water in the Hispanic Southwest,* Professor Michael C. Meyer uses the Arias de Quiros case to show how a provincial governor could add a supplementary water right to an existing land grant (126, 133). For his example, Meyer relied on SANM I, no. 8, a copy of the 1715 proceedings made circa 1830 on orders from the villa's alcalde constitucional, José Ignacio Ortiz. That document does not include Governor Martínez's disavowal of the *merced* made by his predecessor. Taken from the cabildo archives, SANM I, no. 169 covers the entire affair.

7. SANM II, no. 317a, Criminal proceedings against Nicolás Ortiz, Santa Fe, 1723.

8. Ibid.

9. SG, no. 65, Juan de Gabaldón Grant.

10. Ortiz to Concha, April 22 and May 2, 1788. Translations of these documents were sent December 26, 1923 to Commissioner of Indian Affairs Charles H. Burke by Ralph Emerson Twitchell, a Santa Fe lawyer and historian then serving as special assistant to the attorney general, National Archives, Record Group 75, Records of the Office of Indian Affairs, Letters Received, Central Files, 1907–1939, T-01978.

11. Eleanor B. Adams and Fray Angelico Chavez, *The Missions of New Mexico, 1776: A Description by Fray Francisco Atanasio Domínguez with Other Contemporary Documents* (Albuquerque, 1956): 41, 51.

12. Santa Fe County Deed Records, Book S: 130–32, Office of the County Clerk, Santa Fe

County Courthouse, Santa Fe, N.M. The entire proceedings were recorded December 26, 1887.

13. SANM II, no. 379, Complaint by citizens of Albuquerque against Cristóbal García regarding an acequia through their lands, 1733.

14. Ibid.

15. SANM II, no. 2600, Complaint of Mariano Martín v. Manuel Martín, 1815. For further adjudication of this lawsuit, see Malcolm Ebright, "Manuel Martínez's Ditch Dispute: A Study in Mexican Period Custom and Justice," *New Mexico Historical Review* 54 (January 1979): 21–34.

16. SANM I, no. 614, Diego Antonio Martín, complaint concerning damages caused by an acequia, Santa Cruz, 1819;, SANM II, no. 2738, Index of judicial cases, August 5, 1818–February 17, 1824, no. 58.

17. Rio Arriba County Records, Deed Book 2: 286–87, SRCA. This volume has been photocopied from the original.

18. Taos County Deed Records, Book A-5: 253–63. This volume, sometimes identified as E-5, is no longer in official custody. Martín's petition and Ortiz's response were added to a copy of the Don Fernando de Taos land grant papers that were recorded by County Clerk Santiago Valdez on July 20, 1876. A transcript of the documents is found in an abstract of title prepared by Northern New Mexico Abstract Co., Taos, N.M., June 5, 1968, located in files of the State Engineer Office, Santa Fe, N.M.

19. SANM I, no. 954, Bartolomé Trujillo and others, grant of lands on the Rio Chama at Abiquiú, 1734.

20. J. Richard Salazar, "Santa Rosa de Lima de Abiquiú," *New Mexico Architecture* 18 (September–October 1976): 16; SG no. 149, Plaza Colorada Grant.

21. SANM I, no. 847, Miguel Martín Serrano, proceedings against los Valdeses, Abiquiú, 1746.

22. For recent photographic evidence of the Chama's inexorable shift to the south, see Salazar, "Santa Rosa de Lima de Abiquiú": 19.

23. Martín and Martín to Chacón, June 13, 1797, Pablo Gonzales Papers, Newberry Library, Chicago, Ill., microfilm copy, SRCA.

24. Decree of Lieutenant Juan Antonio Barela, Santa Rosa de Abiquiú, August 30, 1806, Silvanio Salazar Collection, SRCA.

25. SANM II, no. 465c, Proceedings against Manuel Valerio for mistreatment of Juan Antonio Salazar, Santa Cruz, 1745.

26. SANM II, no. 2846, Case against Manuel Vigil, Chimayó, 1819.

27. SANM II, no. 1368, Case against Juan Ignacio Vigil, Santa Fe, 1796. For some comments on *caución juratoria,* see Elizabeth Howard West, "The Right of Asylum in New Mexico in the Seventeenth and Eighteenth Centuries," *New Mexico Historical Review* 41 (April 1966): 118, 120, 138–39, 142.

28. SANM II, no. 1401 and 1469, Chacón to Audencia of Guadalajara, 1797 and 1799. For discussion of the *indulto,* see Cutter, "Judicial Practice in New Spain,": 221–23.

29. Cutter, "Judicial Practice in New Spain": 207–08, 236.

## Chapter 3

1. Oakah L. Jones Jr., *Los Paisanos: Spanish Settlers on the Northern Frontier of New Spain* (Norman, 1979):125–29, 141; Spanish Archives of New Mexico (SANM) II, no. 2705, New Mexico Census Summary, 1817, State Records Center and Archives (SRCA), Santa Fe, N.M.

2. Mexican Archives of New Mexico (MANM), Communications of Local Officials, *Informe que da el jues suplente de paz,* 1840, SRCA.

3. Ibid.

4. Marc Simmons, *Spanish Government in New Mexico* (Albuquerque, 1968): 166–67, 193 n.3, 205, 211–12; Charles R. Cutter, "Judicial Practice in New Spain, 1700–1810," Ph.D.

diss., University of New Mexico, 1989: 29–30, 141–42; Michael C. Meyer, *Water in the Hispanic Southwest: A Social and Legal History* (Tucson, 1984): 157.

5. MANM, Legislative Proceedings, Elections—Ayuntamientos, Taos, 1833.

6. For a discussion of settlement and population growth in the Taos area, see John O. Baxter, *Spanish Irrigation in Taos Valley*, State Engineer Office (Santa Fe, 1990): 5–19. The 1821 census summary is found in SANM II, no. 3094.

7. Records of the Surveyor General of New Mexico (SG), no. 159, Arroyo Hondo Grant, SRCA; Baxter, *Spanish Irrigation in Taos Valley:* 23–27.

8. For the Máynez merced, see SANM I, no. 389, Juan Eusebio García de la Mora, question of lands at Taos, 1826.

9. SG no. 159, Arroyo Hondo Grant. The ayuntamiento's decision is appended to a copy of the act of possession made by Alcalde Juan Antonio Lovato, July 23, 1823, identified as "Exhibit B."

10. SANM I, no. 1292, Pueblo of Taos and others v. residents of Arroyo Seco over waters from the Rio Lucero, 1823. For comments on this case, see Meyer, *Water in the Hispanic Southwest:* 54–55, 139, 160; Daniel Tyler, *The Mythical Pueblo Rights Doctrine: Water Administration in Hispanic New Mexico* (El Paso, 1990): 35–36; Charles T. DuMars, Marilyn O'Leary, Albert E. Utton, *Pueblo Indian Water Rights: Struggle for a Precious Resource* (Tucson, 1984): 127–28. The definition of a surco was provided by Mr. Fermín Torres, commissioner of La Acequia Madre del Rio Lucero del Arroyo Seco, personal communication, September 17, 1987.

11. Territorial District Court Records, Taos County Civil Case no. 343, *Juan R. Quintana et al. v. Juan de León et al.*, August 3, 1887, transcript of testimony: 11, 21–22, SRCA. The original transcript is missing from the case file at the Records Center, but a copy is found in Legal Files, Pueblo of Taos, Southern Pueblos Agency, Albuquerque, N.M.

12. SG no. 86, La Talaya Grant.

13. SANM I, no. 628, José Vitorino Montes Vigil, Claim to land on the Rio Lucero, 1836–1837.

14. SG no. 58, Rio Grande del Rancho Grant.

15. MANM, Legislative Records, Santa Fe ayuntamiento proceedings, May 9, 1829, April 12, 1832.

16. José María Chaves Papers, Box 1, *Abiendo reclamado los cuidadanos de la plaza de Nuestra Señora de Guadalupe*, Abiquiú, May 6, 1828, Newberry Library, Chicago, Ill., microfilm copy, SRCA.

17. Rio Arriba County Deed Book 3: 95–97, Office of the County Clerk, Rio Arriba County Courthouse, Tierra Amarilla, N.M.

18. Rio Ariba County Deed Book 3: 89–94.

19. MANM, Governor's Papers, Letterbook of communications sent to officials within New Mexico, January 2, 1832–August 8, 1833, July 9 and 13, 1833. Residence of the litigants is found in a census of Santa Cruz de la Cañada and its environs, Archives of the Archdiocese of Santa Fe, Loose Documents, 1822, no. 30, Census of Santa Cruz de la Cañada.

20. The original ayuntamiento decision is found in the Kenneth D. Sender Collection, no. 121, SRCA. A copy is located in MANM, Legislative Records, Ayuntamiento Proceedings, Santa Cruz de la Cañada, August 4, 1833. For a similar right-of-way dispute at Abiquiú, see Malcolm Ebright, "Manuel Martinez's Ditch Dispute: A Study in Mexican Period Custom and Justice," *New Mexico Historical Review* 54 (January 1979): 21–34.

21. SANM I, no. 395, José Victor García, proceedings against Juan Rafael Ortiz, 1831–1832.

22. Documentation from an 1844 case at Santa Cruz indicated that those selected as hombres buenos must be over twenty-five years old and capable of exercising the rights of citizens. MANM, Communications of Local Officials, April 12, 1844. Functions and

responsibilities of hombres buenos in Mexican California are discussed in David J. Langum, *Law and Community on the Mexican California Frontier: Anglo-American Expatriates and the Clash of Legal Traditions, 1821–1846* (Norman, 1987): 87–88, 97–98. Langum insists that the "good men" were not advocates, but, in New Mexico, they frequently attempted to advance the interests of their clients.

23. SANM I, no. 395.

24. Santa Fe County Deed Book O: 544–45, Office of the County Clerk, Santa Fe, County Courthouse, Santa Fe, N.M. For a similar arrangement at Belén in the Rio Abajo, see an agreement between the Acequia de los Garcías and Acequia de los Pueblitos, February 17, 1832, Valencia County Deed Book E-4: 206–07, SRCA.

25. Santa Fe County Deed Book A-1: 56.

26. Córdova Family Papers, Juan Lorenzo Torres v. Juan de Jesús Lopes, May 15, 1834, SRCA.

27. Records of both incidents are found in MANM, Judicial Proceedings, Jurisdiction of Santa Cruz de la Cañada, Alcalde of Chama, Book of Verbal Decisions, March 28 and August 1, 1835.

28. Taos County Deed Book A-8: 30, Office of the County Clerk, Taos County Courthouse, Taos, N.M.

29. Santa Fe County Deed Book S: 136–37.

30. MANM, Judicial Proceedings, Petition of José Miguel Aragón, July 9, 1827.

31. Ibid, Complaint against Santiago Ulibarrí, August 7, 1827.

32. Ibid, Complaint against residents of San Miguel del Bado, March 28–April 2, 1824.

33. A copy of this document was found in the Rio Arriba County records and transferred to the State Records Center and Archives in Santa Fe where it is filed under "Miscellaneous Land Grants." On July 5, 1853, it was recorded in Rio Arriba County Deed Book 1: 42.

34. Rio Arriba County Deed Book 1: 44–47.

35. Rio Arriba County Deed Book 1: 47–49.

36. For a concise summary of governmental changes under the centralists, see David J. Weber, *The Mexican Frontier, 1821–1846: The American Southwest under Mexico* (Albuquerque, 1982): 33–35.

37. Langum, *Law and Community on the California Frontier:* 38, 97–98.

38. MANM, Communications of Local Officials, Santa Cruz de la Cañada, April 12, 1844; Santa Fe County Deed Book E-1: 167.

39. Sender Collection, no. 200, *Juan Ricardo Martínez v. Rafael García*, San Antonio de Chama, April 19, 1838.

40. MANM, Miscellaneous Communications, Gallegos and Luna to prefect of first district, December 1, 1841.

41. Ibid.

42. Sender Collection, no. 266, Records of the Justice of the Peace, Jurisdiction of Santa Clara, *Juan de Jesús Córdova v. José Rafael Trujillo*, April 5–July 21, 1841. A copy of these proceedings is found in SANM I, no. 225, Córdova v. Trujillo, April 5, 1841–August 10, 1844.

43. Sender Collection, no. 279, Trujillo to Archuleta, February 16, 1843.

44. SANM I, no. 225, Antonio Enrique Córdova to Archuleta, March 7, 1843.

45. Sender Collection, no. 285, decree of Juez de Paz Rafael García, April 28, 1843. A copy is found in SANM I, no. 225.

46. SANM I, no. 225, Córdova to Martínez, July 23, 1844 and Martínez decree, August 3, 1844.

47. Sender Collection, no. 203, *Jesús María Manzanares v. Pedro de Herrera*, September 3–27, 1838.

## Chapter 4

1. See Ralph Emerson Twitchell, *The Leading Facts of New Mexican History*, 5 vols. (Cedar Rapids, 1911–1917), 2: 199–261.

2. Lewis H. Garrard, *Wah-To-Yah and the Taos Trail*, ed. Ralph P. Bieber (Glendale, 1943): 232–33.

3. Ibid.: 245–46.

4. A copy of the questionnaire is found in "Report of the Commissioner of Patents for the Year 1852, Part II, Agriculture," *Senate Executive Document 55, 32nd Congress, 2nd Session* (Serial 667): 58–60.

5. For Alvarez's long career in New Mexico, see Thomas E. Chávez, *Manuel Alvarez, 1794–1856: A Southwestern Biography* (Niwot, 1990). An account of Baird's agricultural activities is found in Marc Simmons, *Albuquerque: A Narrative History* (Albuquerque, 1982): 155–59. A native of South Carolina, Hammond served a tour of duty at San Francisco's presidio after he left New Mexico. Part of his farm report was included in "A statistical report on the sickness and mortality in the Army of the United States . . . from January, 1839, to January, 1855," *Senate Executive Document 96, 34th Congress, 1st Session* (Serial 827), republished as John Fox Hammond, *A Surgeon Reports on Socorro, New Mexico, 1852* (Santa Fe, 1966). Biographical notes concerning Massie appear in Donald Chaput, *François X. Aubry: Trader, Trailmaker and Voyageur of the Southwest 1846–1854* (Glendale, 1975): 196.

6. The following discussion is taken from "Report of the Commissioner of Patents, 1851, Part II, Agriculture," *Senate Executive Document 118, 32nd Congress, 1st Session* (Serial 625): 478–92 and "Report of the Commissioner of Patents for the Year 1852, Part II, Agriculture,": 345–52.

7. *Organic Law of the Territory of New Mexico,* 1846, Library, Division of History, Museum of New Mexico, Santa Fe, N.M.: 3–12, 38–45, 114. A facsimile edition has been published by Nolie Mumey (Santa Fe, 1970).

8. Robert W. Larson, *New Mexico's Quest for Statehood, 1846–1912,* (Albuquerque, 1968): 5–6, 55–57.

9. *Organic Act Establishing the Territory of New Mexico,* September 9, 1850, reprinted in Richard N. Ellis, ed., *New Mexico Historic Documents* (Albuquerque, 1975): 32–38.

10. James J. Deavenport, ed., *Revised Statutes of the Territory of New Mexico* (Santa Fe, 1856): 286–88.

11. L. Bradford Prince, ed., *The General Laws of New Mexico Including All the Unrepealed General Laws from the Promulgation of the "Kearney [sic] Code" in 1846, to the End of the Legislative Session of 1880* (Albany, 1882): 14–16.

12. San Miguel County Justice of the Peace Record Book, 1858–1870 (n.p.; see entries for April 7, 1867, July 16, 1859, September 15, 1865, and June 22, 1866), SRCA.

13. Valencia County Deed Book E-4: 171–73, SRCA.

14. For comments on powers exercised by probate judges in the early territorial period, see Howard Roberts Lamar, *The Far Southwest, 1846–1912: A Territorial History* (New Haven, 1966): 85–86.

15. Taos County Probate Proceedings, Book C-1: 110, Book C-2: 1, SRCA. Long's family is included in Fray Angélico Chavez, "New Names in New Mexico, 1820–1850," *El Palacio* 64 (September, October 1957): 315–16.

16. Taos County Probate Proceedings, Book C-1: 140–41.

17. Taos County Probate Proceedings, Book C-2: 433–35.

18. Taos County Probate Proceedings, Book C-3: 13–14.

19. Taos County Probate Proceedings, Book C-5: 330–33.

20. Ibid.: 334–35, 337–38.

21. Taos County Probate Proceedings, Book C-4: 276.

22. Taos County Probate Proceedings, Book C-5: 267–69, 272.

23. San Miguel County Probate Court Record Book, 1847–1853: 34, SRCA.

24. Santa Ana County Probate Proceedings, 1864–1876: 13, 55, 73–75, SRCA.

25. Valencia County Probate Court Records, 1848–1856: 19, SRCA.

26. Ibid.: 121.

27. Taos County Probate Proceedings, Book C-5: 198.

28. San Miguel County Probate Journal, 1863–1873: 66.

29. Taos County Probate Proceedings, Book C-6: 231–35.

30. Taos County Probate Proceedings, Book C-5: 187–90. Although less concerned with water conservation, settlers at Refugio La Unión, a community west of the Rio Grande about thirty miles south of Las Cruces, also adopted a plan to protect their timber. At a public meeting on February 2, 1875, residents expressed outrage that strangers from El Paso and across the border in Mexico were cutting firewood, vigas, and latillas from their bosques without paying compensation. To protect local groves, they voted to hire a *bosquero* empowered to charge a small fee for each cartload of firewood or building materials hauled off by outsiders. See Doña Ana County Records, Miscellaneous, February 2, 1875, SRCA.

31. Prince, ed., *The General Laws of New Mexico:* 13–16.

32. Ira G. Clark, *Water in New Mexico: A History of its Management and Use* (Albuquerque, 1987): 25.

33. William A. Keleher, *Turmoil in New Mexico, 1846–1868* (Santa Fe, 1952): 383.

34. *Local and Special Laws of New Mexico, 1884* (Santa Fe, 1885): 20–25.

35. Ibid.: 614–19.

36. Ibid.: 130–33.

37. Ibid.: 426–29. Although legislation for this project proved premature, it was developed after the turn of the century by J. D. Hand, president of the Placita Ranch Co., who owned most of the irrigable lands in the area and was able to raise Eastern capital. See Water Rights Files, Edward F. Shellaberger, no. 91 (cancelled) and 244, State Engineer Office, Santa Fe, N.M.

38. *Local and Special Laws of New Mexico, 1884:* 478–81, 494–99. A proposal to dam Santa Fe's river had been made as early as 1847 after New Mexico's acting governor, Donaciano Vigil, had requested two U.S. Army officers, Lieutenants J. F. Gilmer and R. C. Garnier, to make recommendations for increasing the town's water supply. Their report was printed in the *Santa Fe Republican,* October 1, 1847.

39. *Local and Special Laws of New Mexico, 1884:* 630–31. While dampening the controversy for some years, this bill failed to resolve the apportionment problem. As recently as 1956, Los Córdovas residents claimed that mayordomos upstream denied them a fair share of the river. The parties negotiated an out-of-court settlement on that occasion, however. See Water Rights Files, Los Córdovas Ditch No. 1, No. 0942.

40. *Local and Special Laws of New Mexico, 1884:* 114–15.

41. Ibid.: 52–54.

42. Ibid.: 312–15.

43. Ibid.: 286–87.

44. Ibid.: 340–43.

45. Ibid.: 550–51.

46. Taos County Deed Records, Book A-9: 440, Office of the County Clerk, Taos County Courthouse, Taos, N.M.

47. Ibid.: 121.

48. Taos County Deed Records, Book A-10: 174–75.

49. Valencia County Deed Records, Book A-4: 788–91, Office of the County Clerk, Valencia County Courthouse, Los Lunas, N.M.

50. Valencia County Deed Records, Book A-7: 462–63.

51. Taos County Deed Records, Book A-20: 224–25.

52. Taos County Deed Records, Book A-1: 171–72, SRCA. Books A-1 through A-6 are now in state custody. All other volumes in this series remain in the county clerk's office of the Taos County Courthouse.

53. For examples at Embudo and Santa Cruz, see Rio Arriba County Deed Records, Book 9: 351, 413, Office of the County Clerk, Rio Arriba County Courthouse, Tierra Amarilla, N.M.

54. Bernalillo County Deed Records, Book F: 350–51, microfilm copy, SRCA.

## Chapter 5

1. Arthur H. Frazier and Wilbur Heckler, *Embudo, New Mexico, Birthplace of Systematic Stream Gaging,* U.S. Geological Survey Professional Paper 778 (Washington, 1972): 1–6.

2. For Powell's career, see William Culp Darrah, *Powell of the Colorado* (Princeton, 1951) and Wallace Stegner, *Beyond the Hundredth Meridian* (Boston, 1954).

3. Frazier and Heckler, *Embudo, New Mexico:* 5–8, 17–20.

4. "Twelfth Annual Report of the Director of the United States Geological Survey, Part II, Irrigation," *House Executive Document 1, Part 5, 52nd Congress, 1st Session* (Serial 2937): 273; F. H. Newell, *Report on Agriculture by Irrigation in the Western Part of the United States at the Eleventh Census: 1890* (Washington, 1894): 193–94.

5. "Twelfth Annual Report": 254, 272–73, 288; Newell, *Report on Agriculture:* 194–96, 199.

6. "Twelfth Annual Report": 272–73; Newell, *Report on Agriculture:* 194.

7. Ibid: 196. Despite great potential, both projects had difficulty attracting settlers. See Jim Berry Pearson, *The Maxwell Land Grant* (Norman, 1961): 145–56, 223.

8. Newell, *Report on Agriculture:* 198.

9. Ibid.: 195, 200; "Twelfth Annual Report": 253, 279–80.

10. Howard Roberts Lamar, *The Far Southwest, 1845–1912: A Territorial History* (New Haven, 1966): 107.

11. Jack E. Holmes, *Politics in New Mexico* (Albuquerque, 1967): 9.

12. *Thirteenth Census of the United States taken in the year 1910, Abstract of the Census with Supplement for New Mexico* (Washington, 1913): 568.

13. David F. Myrick, *New Mexico's Railroads: An Historical Survey* (Golden, 1970): 17–18.

14. Jim F. Heath, "A Study of the Influence of the Atchison, Topeka and Santa Fe Railroad on the Economy of New Mexico, 1878–1900," unpublished MA thesis, University of New Mexico, 1955: 44; Ralph Emerson Twitchell, *The Leading Facts of New Mexican History,* 5 vols. (Cedar Rapids, 1911–1917), 2: 482.

15. Heath, "Influence of the Atchison, Topeka and Santa Fe": 41–42, 46–48, 72.

16. William H. Goetzmann, *Exploration and Empire: The Explorer and the Scientist in the Winning of the American West* (New York, 1966): 573. For Powell's report, see *House Executive Document 73, 45th Congress, 2nd Session* (Serial 1805).

17. Goetzmann, *Exploration and Empire:* 572–74, 596–99; Ira G. Clark, *Water in New Mexico: A History of its Management and Use* (Albuquerque, 1987): 56–59; Frazier and Heckler, *Embudo, New Mexico:* 3–4.

18. Quoted in Heath, "Influence of the Atchison, Topeka and Santa Fe": 85–86.

19. *Reports of Committees of the Senate of the United States, 1889–'90,* no. 928, Special Committee on Irrigation, *51st Congress, 1st Session* (Serial 2708), Part 3: 65–68, 77–78, 81–84.

20. *Acts of the Legislative Assembly of the Territory of New Mexico, Twenty-Seventh Session* (Las Vegas, 1887): 29–37.

21. Lamar, *The Far Southwest:* 85; L. Bradford Prince, ed., *The General Laws of New*

*Mexico Including All the Unrepealed General Laws from the Promulgation of the "Kearney Code"* in 1846, to the End of the Legislative Session of 1880 (Albany, 1882): 222–33.

22. *Compiled Laws of New Mexico, 1897* (Santa Fe, 1897): 320–21. Curiously, the legislature, in 1882, noted the confusion surrounding water issues after creation of the county commissioners and passed a law ordering probate judges to maintain jurisdiction of "streams of water and the distribution thereof," with the proviso that the act applied only to Taos County. *Local and Special Laws of New Mexico, 1884* (Santa Fe, 1885): 630–31.

23. For biographical information concerning the territorial judiciary, see Twitchell, *Leading Facts of New Mexican History*, 2: passim.

24. Territorial District Court Records (TDCR), Taos County Civil Case no. 343, *Juan R. Quintana et al. v. Juan de León et al.*, August 3, 1887, State Records Center and Archives (SRCA), Santa Fe, N.M.

25. TDCR, Taos County Civil Case no. 446, *Francisco Martínez y Martínez et al. v. Melaquias Martínez et al.*, July 6, 1893, bill of complaint, Edward L. Bartlett Papers, SRCA.

26. Taos County Civil Case no. 446, Record Book A: 400, 402.

27. TDCR, Taos County Civil Case no. 269, *José Martín et al. v. Leandro Martínez et al.*, April 13, 1883.

28. TDCR, Taos County civil Case no. 492, *Linton M. Cutter v. Samuel Johnson et al.*, June 19, 1896, Docket Book 1: 258. The apportionment is found in Water Rights Files, Lobo Creek, no. 0185, State Engineer Office, Santa Fe, N.M.

29. TDCR, Taos County Civil Case no. 722, *Alexander Gusdorf et al. v. La Acequia del Llano et al.*, December 29, 1903.

30. TDCR, Valencia County Civil Case no. 1411, *Louis Huning v. Adolfo Chávez and Patrocino Córdova*, March 28, 1899.

31. TDCR, Rio Arriba County Civil Case no. 367, *Territory of New Mexico ex rel Esquipula Rodríguez v. José Dolores López*, June 18, 1887.

32. TDCR, Taos County Civil Case no. 679, *Acequia del Llano del Rio Chiquito et al. v. Antonio Valerio*, February 7, 1903.

33. TDCR, Valencia County Civil Case no. 1419, *Jesús H. Sánchez v. Rómulo Aragón, Jesús Sánchez y Alarid et al.*, July 25, 1899.

34. TDCR, Doña Ana County Civil Case no. 1728, *Charles V. Mead and José Sierra v. Anastacio Gutiérrez*, February 6, 1892.

35. TDCR, Valencia County Civil Case no. 1067, *Jesús Sánchez y Alarid v. Leandro Abeita*, February 5, 1889.

36. Records of the Surveyor General of New Mexico (SG), no. 42, Antonio Ortiz Grant, SRCA; SG File no. 7, Town of Chaperito Grant.

37. According to one historian, Chaperito residents introduced a claim for their grant as early as 1855, but, for reasons unknown, the surveyor general failed to act. See Victor Westphall, *Mercedes Reales: Hispanic Land Grants of the Upper Rio Grande Region* (Albuquerque, 1983): 224.

38. TDCR, San Miguel County Civil Case no. 3083, *Wilson Waddingham et al. v. Francisco Robledo et al.*, February 7, 1888.

39. For biographical material concerning Waddingham and Day, see David Remley, *Bell Ranch: Cattle Ranching in the Southwest, 1824–1947* (Albuquerque, 1993).

40. San Miguel County Civil Case no. 3083, *Waddingham v. Robledo*.

41. New Mexico Supreme Court Records (SCR), Case no. 435, *Wilson Waddingham et al. v. Francisco Robledo et al.*, January 6, 1892, SRCA.

42. Victor Westphall, *Thomas Benton Catron and His Era* (Tucson, 1973): 62–65.

43. San Miguel County Civil Case no. 3083, *Waddingham v. Robledo*.

44. John F. Zimmerman to Catron, August 15, 1910, Thomas B. Catron Papers (CP), File 103, Box 36, Zimmerman Library, University of New Mexico, Albuquerque, N.M.

45. Charles Hewitt to Catron, November 22, 1910, Mrs. J. T. Blaylock to Catron, March 10, 1911, CP, File 103, Box 36.

46. H. B. Hening to Catron, December 21 and 23, 1910, CP, File 103, Box 36; Westphall, *Thomas Benton Catron:* 65–66.

47. TDCR, Bernalillo County Civil Case no. 4956, *The Albuquerque Land and Irrigation Co. et al. v. Tomás C. Gutiérrez et al.*, January 17, 1898; Case no. 4994, *Same v. Pueblo de Sandía et al.*, February 7, 1898. When transferred to Santa Fe County district court, the cases were renumbered on the docket as 3956 and 3967 respectively.

48. Santa Fe County Civil Case no. 3956, *Albuquerque Land and Irrigation Co. v. Gutiérrez.*

49. McFie's opinion is reprinted in full in SCR, Case no. 858, *Gutiérrez v. Irrigation Co.*, January 1900.

50. Ibid.

51. Myra Ellen Jenkins and Spencer Wilson, "Socorro—Facts Not Fancy," *La Crónica de Nuevo Mexico* 21 (June 1985): 2–3. For a lurid account of vigilante activities at Socorro, see Chester D. Potter, "Reminiscences of the Socorro Vigilantes," Paige W. Christiansen, ed., *New Mexico Historical Review* 40 (January 1965): 23–54.

52. TDCR, Socorro County Civil Case no. 1338, *Juan José Baca et al. v. City of Socorro*, March 31, 1885.

53. Ibid.

54. TDCR, Socorro County Civil Case no. 1330, *L. M. Cox v. Jacinto Gallegos*, March 12, 1885.

55. Socorro County Civil Case no 1338, *Baca v. City of Socorro.*

56. Jenkins and Wilson, "Socorro—Facts Not Fancy": 2–3.

57. SCR, Case no. 1437, *Community Ditches or Acequias of Tularosa Townsite v. Tularosa Community Ditch*, April 1 1910, testimony of Mariano Colmonero, Manuel Ortega, and Francisco Sainz; SCR, Case no. 1662, *State of New Mexico, on relation of Community Ditches or Acequias of Tularosa Township et al. v. Tularosa Community Ditch*, "Motion to Open and Introduce New Testimony," January 15, 1913, microfilm copy, Supreme Court Building, Santa Fe, N.M.

58. Darlis A. Miller, *The California Column in New Mexico* (Albuquerque, 1982): 105–09; Philip J. Rasch, "The Tularosa Ditch War," *New Mexico Historical Review* 43 (July, 1968): 229–35.

59. TDCR, Doña Ana County Civil Case no. 873, *Quirino Maes et al. v. David M. Easton et al.*, June 24, 1885.

60. Westphall, *Thomas Benton Catron:* 68–69; Tularosa Land and Cattle Company, Articles of Incorporation, March 29, 1890, CP, File 608. For biographical profiles of Riley and Rynerson, see William A. Keleher, *Violence in Lincoln County, 1869–1881: A New Mexico Item* (Albuquerque, 1957): 56, 103–04.

61. TDCR, Doña Ana County Civil Case no. 1804, *Tulorosa Land and Cattle Company v. Henry K. Parker et al.*, May 4, 1893.

62. Territorial Archives of New Mexico (TANM), Records of the Secretary of the Territory, Records of Incorporation, Corporation Classification Index, 1868–1910: 65, SRCA.

63. Riley to Catron, January 4, 1905, CP, File 103, Box 22. See also Westphall, *Thomas Benton Catron:* 69.

64. A copy of Judge Mann's decree is found in SCR, Case no. 1437, *Community Ditches v. Tularosa Community Ditch.*

65. George Curry, *George Curry, 1861–1947: An Autobiography*, H. B. Hening, ed. (Albuquerque, 1958): 111.

66. TDCR, Otero County Civil Case no. 937, *Community Ditches or Acequias of Tularosa Townsite v. Tularosa Community Ditch*, April 1, 1910. Almost all the documents from this

case and the supreme court's ruling are found in SCR, Case no. 1437, *Community Ditches v. Tularosa Community Ditch.*

67. SCR, Case no. 1662, *State of N.M. ex rel Community Ditches v. Tularosa Community Ditch.*

68. Doña Ana County District Court Records, Criminal Case no. 5327, *State of New Mexico v. James L. Porter,* October, 1914, SRCA.

69. SCR, Case no. 1662, *State of N.M. ex rel Community Ditches v. Tularosa Community Ditch.*

70. Clark, *Water in New Mexico:* 115–19.

71. For Manby generally, see Myra Ellen Jenkins, "Arthur Rockfort Manby," *The 1966 Brand Book of the Denver Posse of the Westerners* (Boulder, 1967). For a more extended, but not entirely reliable, biography, see Frank Waters, *To Possess the Land: A Biography of Arthur Rockfort Manby* (Chicago: The Swallow Press, 1973).

72. Jenkins, "Arthur Rockfort Manby": 251–54; TDCR, Taos County Civil Case no. 630, *A. R. Manby et al. v. Daniel Martínez et al.,* January 28, 1902.

73. Tabulated List of Proposed Irrigation and Power Projects in New Mexico Compiled from Applications to Appropriate Public Waters, *Second Biennial Report of the Territorial Engineer, 1908–1910,* Records of the State Engineer, folder 1924, SRCA; Claim to Unappropriated Waters, Rio Hondo, Rio Lucero, Arroyo Seco, February 15, 1907, Taos County Miscellaneous Records, Book M-17: 255–56, Office of the County Clerk, Taos County Courthouse, Taos, N.M.

74. Gortner to Manby, May 22, 1907, Napoleon B. Laughlin Papers, Land Grants, file 2, folder 2, SRCA; *Tabulated List, Second Biennial Report of the Territorial Engineer.*

75. Manby to Blanchard, October 5, 1908, TANM, Records of the Territorial Governors, 1846–1912, George Curry Papers, 1907–1910, L/R, SRCA.

# Bibliography

*Archives and Collections*

Archives of the Archdiocese of Santa Fe, Albuquerque
Newberry Library, Chicago
  José María Chaves Papers
  Pablo Gonzales Papers
State Records Center and Archives, Santa Fe (SRCA)
  Administrative Records of New Mexico
    Mexican Archives of New Mexico (MANM)
    Spanish Archives of New Mexico (SANM)
      Series I
      Series II
    Territorial Archives of New Mexico (TANM)
  County Deed Records
    Bernalillo County
    Rio Arriba County
    San Miguel County
    Santa Fe County
    Taos County
    Valencia County
  County Probate Court Records
    Doña Ana County
    San Miguel County
    Santa Ana County
    Taos County
    Valencia County
  Legal Records
    Records of the New Mexico Supreme Court, (SCR)
    Territorial District Court Records, (TDCR)
      Bernalillo County
      Doña Ana County
      Otero County
      Rio Arriba County
      San Miguel County
      Santa Fe County
      Socorro County
      Taos County
      Valencia County

Private Collections
   Edward L. Bartlett Papers
   Napoleon B. Laughlin Papers
   Silvanio Salazar Papers
   Keneth D. Sender Collection
Records of Land Adjudications
   Surveyor General of New Mexico (SG)
   Court of Private Land Claims (PLC)
University of New Mexico, Zimmerman Library, Center for Southwest Research, Albuquerque
   Thomas B. Catron Papers (CP)

## Compilations of Laws

*Acts of the Legislature of the Territory of New Mexico, Twenty-Seventh Session, 1887,* Las Vegas, J. A. Carruth, 1887.
*Compiled Laws of New Mexico, 1897,* Santa Fe, New Mexican Printing Co., 1897.
Deavenport, James J., ed., *Revised Statutes of the Territory of New Mexico,* Santa Fe, 1856.
*Local and Special Laws of New Mexico, 1884,* Santa Fe, New Mexican Printing Co., 1885.
*Organic Law of the Territory of New Mexico,* Santa Fe, 1846.
Prince, L. Bradford, ed., *The General Laws of New Mexico Including All the Unrepealed General Laws from the Promulgation of the "Kearney Code" in 1846, to the End of the Legislative Session of 1880,* Albany, W. C. Little & Co., 1882.

## Records of the New Mexico State Engineer Office, Santa Fe Water Rights Files
## United States Government Documents

Newell, F. H., *Report on Agriculture by Irrigation in the Western Part of the United States at the Eleventh Census: 1890,* Washington, Government Printing Office, 1894.
Powell, John Wesley, "Report on the Lands of the Arid Regions of the United States," *House Executive Document 73, 45th Congress, 2nd Session* (Serial 1805).
"Report of the Commissioner of Patents, 1851, Part II, Agriculture," *Senate Executive Document 118, 32nd Congress, 1st Session* (Serial 625): 478–92.
"Report of the Commissioner of Patents for the Year 1852, Part II, Agriculture," *Senate Executive Document 55, 32nd Congress, 2nd Session* (Serial 667): 345–52.
*Reports of Committees of the Senate of the United States, 1889–90, no. 928,* Special Committee on Irrigation, *51st Congress, 1st Session* (Serial 2708).
*Thirteenth Census of the United States taken in the year 1910, Abstract of the Census with supplement for New Mexico,* Washington, Government Printing Office, 1913.
"Twelfth Annual Report of the Director of the United States Geological Survey, Part II, Irrigation," *House Executive Document 1, Part 5, 52nd Congress, 1st Session* (Serial 2937).

## Books, Articles, and Miscellaneous Works

Adams, Eleanor B. and Fray Angelico Chavez, *The Missions of New Mexico, 1776: A Description by Fray Francisco Atanasio Domínguez with Other Contemporary Documents,* Albuquerque, University of New Mexico Press, 1956.
Baxter, John O., *Spanish Irrigation in the Pojoaque and Tesuque Valleys During the Eighteenth and Early Nineteenth Centuries,* Santa Fe, State Engineer Office, 1984.
———, *Spanish Irrigation in Taos Valley,* Santa Fe, State Engineer Office, 1990.

Chaput, Donald, *François X. Aubry: Trader, Trailmaker and Voyageur in the Southwest, 1846–1854,* Glendale, Arthur H. Clark Co., 1975.

Chavez, Fray Angelico, *Origins of New Mexico Families in the Spanish Colonial Period,* Santa Fe, Historical Society of New Mexico, 1954.

Chávez, Thomas E., *Manuel Alvarez, 1794–1856: A Southwestern Biography,* Niwot, University of Colorado Press, 1990.

Chevalier, François, *Land and Society in Colonial Mexico: The Great Hacienda,* Berkeley, University of California Press, 1970.

Clark, Ira G., *Water in New Mexico: A History of its Management and Use,* Albuquerque, University of New Mexico Press, 1987.

Curry, George, *George Curry, 1861–1947: An Autobiography,* H. B. Hening, ed., Albuquerque, University of New Mexico Press, 1958.

Cutter, Charles R., "Judicial Practice in New Spain, 1700–1810," Ph.D. diss., University of New Mexico, 1989.

Darrah, William Culp, *Powell of the Colorado,* Princeton, Princeton University Press, 1951.

DuMars, Charles T., Marilyn O'Leary, Albert E. Utton, *Pueblo Indian Water Rights: Struggle for a Precious Resource,* Tucson, University of Arizona Press, 1984.

Ebright, Malcolm, "Manuel Martínez's Ditch Dispute: A Study in Mexican Period Custom and Justice," *New Mexico Historical Review,* vol. 54 (1979): 21–34.

Ellis, Richard N., ed., *New Mexico Historic Documents,* Albuquerque, University of New Mexico Press, 1975.

Espinosa, J. Manuel, *Crusaders of the Rio Grande: The Story of Don Diego de Vargas and the Reconquest and Refounding of New Mexico,* Chicago, Institute of Jesuit History, 1942.

———, *First Expedition of Vargas into New Mexico, 1692,* Albuquerque, University of New Mexico Press, 1940.

Frazier, Arthur H. and Wilbur Heckler, *Embudo, New Mexico, Birthplace of Systematic Stream Gaging,* Washington, U.S. Geological Survey Professional Paper 778, 1972.

Garrard, Lewis H., *Wah-To-Yah and the Taos Trail,* Ralph P. Bieber, ed., Glendale, Arthur H. Clark Co., 1943.

Gibson, Charles, *The Aztecs Under Spanish Rule, A History of the Indians of the Valley of Mexico, 1519–1810,* Stanford, Stanford University Press, 1964.

Goetzmann, William H., *Exploration and Empire: The Explorer and the Scientist in the Winning of the American West,* New York, Alfred A. Knopf, 1966.

Hackett, Charles Wilson, ed., *Historical Documents Relating to New Mexico, Nueva Viscaya and Approaches Thereto, to 1773, Collected by Adolph F. A. Bandelier and Fanny R. Bandelier,* 3 vols., Washington, Carnegie Institution, 1923–1937.

———, ed., and Charmion Clair Shelby, tr., *Revolt of the Pueblo Indians of New Mexico and Otermín's Attempted Reconquest, 1680–1682,* 2 vols., Albuquerque, University of New Mexico Press, 1953.

Hammond, George P., and Agapito Rey, *Don Juan de Oñate, Colonizer of New Mexico, 1595–1628,* 2 vols., Albuquerque, University of New Mexico Press, 1953.

Hammond, John Fox, *A Surgeon Reports on Socorro, New Mexico, 1852,* Santa Fe, Stagecoach Press, 1966.

Heath, Jim F., "A Study of the Influence of the Atchison, Topeka and Santa Fe Railroad on the Economy of New Mexico, 1878–1900," MA thesis, University of New Mexico, 1955.

Holmes, Jack E., *Politics in New Mexico*, Albuquerque, University of New Mexico Press, 1967.

Jenkins, Myra Ellen, "Arthur Rockfort Manby," *The 1966 Brand Book of the Denver Posse of the Westerners*, Boulder, 1967.

—— and John O. Baxter, "Settlement and Irrigation in the Santa Cruz-Quemado Watershed," Santa Fe, State Engineer Office, 1986.

—— and Spencer Wilson, "Socorro—Facts Not Fancy," *La Crónica de Nuevo México*, no. 20 and 21, 1985.

John, Elizabeth A. H., *Storms Brewed in Other Men's Worlds: The Confrontation of Indians, Spanish, and French in the Southwest, 1540–1795*, College Station, Texas A & M University Press, 1975.

Jones, Oakah L. Jr., *Los Paisanos: Spanish Settlers on the Northern Frontier of New Spain*, Norman, University of Oklahoma Press, 1979.

Keleher, William A., *Turmoil in New Mexico, 1846–1868*, Santa Fe, Rydal Press, 1952.

——, *Violence in Lincoln County, 1869–1881: A New Mexico Item*, Albuquerque, University of New Mexico Press, 1957.

Lamar, Howard Roberts, *The Far Southwest, 1846–1912: A Territorial History*, New Haven, Yale University Press, 1966.

Langum, David J., *Law and Community on the Mexican California Frontier: Anglo-American Expatriates and the Clash of Legal Traditions, 1821–1846*, Norman, University of Oklahoma Press, 1987.

Larson, Robert W., *New Mexico's Quest for Statehood, 1846–1912*, Albuquerque, University of New Mexico Press, 1968.

McNitt, Frank, *Navajo Wars: Military Campaigns, Slave Raids and Reprisals*, Albuquerque, University of New Mexico Press, 1972.

Meyer, Michael C., *Water in the Hispanic Southwest: A Social and Legal History, 1550–1850*, Tucson, University of Arizona Press, 1984.

Miller, Darlis A., *The California Column in New Mexico*, Albuquerque, University of New Mexico Press, 1982.

Murphy, Michael E., *Irrigation in the Bajío Region of Colonial Mexico*, Boulder, Westview Press, 1986.

Myrick, David F., *New Mexico's Railroads: An Historical Survey*, Golden, Colorado Railroad Museum, 1970.

Pearson, Jim Berry, *The Maxwell Land Grant*, Norman, University of Oklahoma Press, 1961.

Potter, Chester D., "Reminiscences of the Socorro Vigilantes," *New Mexico Historical Review*, vol. 40 (1965): 23–54.

Rasch, Philip J., "The Tularosa Ditch War," *New Mexico Historical Review*, vol. 43 (1968): 229–35.

Reeve, Frank D., "The Navajo-Spanish Peace: 1720s–1770s," *New Mexico Historical Review*, vol. 34 (1959): 9–40.

Remley, David, *Bell Ranch: Cattle Ranching in the Southwest, 1824–1947*, Albuquerque, University of New Mexico Press, 1993.

Salazar, J. Richard, "Santa Rosa de Lima de Abiquiú," *New Mexico Architecture*, vol. 18 (1976): 13–19.

Simmons, Marc, *Albuquerque: A Narrative History*, Albuquerque, University of New Mexico Press, 1982.

——, *Spanish Government in New Mexico*, Albuquerque, University of New Mexico Press, 1968.

Stegner, Wallace, *Beyond the Hundredth Meridian,* Boston, Houghton, Mifflin, 1954.

Thomas, Alfred Barnaby, *After Coronado: Spanish Exploration Northeast of New Mexico, 1696–1727,* Norman, University of Oklahoma Press, 1935.

Torquemada, Juan de, *Monarquía Indiana,* 3 vols., Quinta Edición, Mexico, Editorial Porrúa, S. A., 1975.

Twitchell, Ralph Emerson, *The Leading Facts of New Mexican History,* 5 vols., Cedar Rapids, Torch Press, 1911–1917.

Tyler, Daniel, *The Mythical Pueblo Rights Doctrine: Water Administration in Hispanic New Mexico,* El Paso, Texas Western Press, 1990.

Warner, Ted J., "Don Félix Martínez and the Santa Fe Presidio, 1693–1730," *New Mexico Historical Review,* vol. 45 (1970): 269–310.

Weber, David J., *The Mexican Frontier, 1821–1846: The American Southwest Under Mexico,* Albuquerque, University of New Mexico Press, 1982.

West, Elizabeth Howard, "The Right of Asylum in New Mexico in the Seventeenth and Eighteenth Centuries," *New Mexico Historical Review,* vol. 41 (1966): 115–54.

West, Robert C., *The Mining Community in Northern New Spain: The Parral Mining District, Ibero-Americana,* vol. 30, Berkeley and Los Angeles, University of California Publications, 1949.

Westphall, Victor, *Mercedes Reales: Hispanic Land Grants of the Upper Rio Grande Region,* Albuquerque, University of New Mexico Press, 1983.

———, *Thomas Benton Catron and His Era,* Tucson, University of Arizona Press, 1973.

# Index